Dennis J. Cahill

Lifestyle Market Segmentation

Lifestyle Market Segmentation

THE HAWORTH PRESS
Haworth Series in Segmented, Targeted,
and Customized Marketing: Conceptual
and Empirical Development
Art Weinstein
Editor

Handbook of Market Segmentation: Strategic Targeting for Business and Technology Firms, Third Edition by Art Weinstein

Handbook of Niche Marketing: Principles and Practice edited by Tevfik Dalgic

Lifestyle Market Segmentation by Dennis J. Cahill

Segmentation Strategies for Hospitality Managers: Target Marketing for Competitive Advantage by Ron Morritt

Lifestyle Market Segmentation

Dennis J. Cahill

The Haworth Press
New York • London • Oxford

For more information on this book or to order, visit
http://www.haworthpress.com/store/product.asp?sku=5560

or call 1-800-HAWORTH (800-429-6784) in the United States and Canada
or (607) 722-5857 outside the United States and Canada

or contact orders@HaworthPress.com

The Haworth Press, Inc., 10 Alice Street, Binghamton, NY 13904-1580.

PUBLISHER'S NOTE
The development, preparation, and publication of this work has been undertaken with great care. However, the Publisher, employees, editors, and agents of The Haworth Press are not responsible for any errors contained herein or for consequences that may ensue from use of materials or information contained in this work. The Haworth Press is committed to the dissemination of ideas and information according to the highest standards of intellectual freedom and the free exchange of ideas. Statements made and opinions expressed in this publication do not necessarily reflect the views of the Publisher, Directors, management, or staff of The Haworth Press, Inc., or an endorsement by them.

Cover design by Kerry E. Mack.
TR: 9.21.06

Library of Congress Cataloging-in-Publication Data

Cahill, Dennis J.
Lifestyle market segmentation / Dennis J. Cahill.
p. cm.
Includes bibliographical references and index.
ISBN-13: 978-0-7890-2868-6 (hard : alk. paper)
ISBN-10: 0-7890-2868-9 (hard : alk. paper)
ISBN-13: 978-0-7890-2869-3 (soft : alk. paper)
ISBN-10: 0-7890-2869-7 (soft : alk. paper)
1. Market segmentation. 2. Consumers' preferences. 3. Consumer behavior. 4. Lifestyles. I. Title.

HF5415.127.C34 2006
658.8'02—dc22

2005034927

For my children
Abigail and Teddy

ABOUT THE AUTHOR

Dennis J. Cahill has headed North Union Associates, Inc., a finance, investment, and marketing consulting firm in Cleveland, Ohio, since 1983. He founded the firm after almost a decade of increasingly responsible financial positions held in the cement and banking industries. Mr. Cahill has also taught undergraduate and graduate marketing and finance courses at four Cleveland area colleges. He is the author of *Squeezing a New Service into a Crowded Market, Internal Marketing: Your Company's Next Stage of Growth,* and *How Consumers Pick a Hotel: Strategic Segmentation and Target Marketing* (all published by The Haworth Press, Inc.). He has also published numerous articles in scholarly and professional publications and spoken at national professional conferences and local meetings. While heading North Union Associates, Mr. Cahill has been active in many aspects of new product and new service development, from initial concept through delivery of completed product to end user. He is a member of the American Marketing Association, the Academy of Management, the Association of Psychological Type, the Association for Consumer Research, the Cleveland Business Economists Club, and The Barnard Society, USA.

CONTENTS

Foreword

It's hard to imagine finding anyone more qualified than Dennis Cahill to author a book on the very latest in Lifestyle Market Segmentation.

If I may mix a metaphor, here is a guy who has walked the talk and now talks the walk. For he has been ever-present on every side of the segmentation equation: as academic, as researcher, and as practitioner in a most hands-on manner, crafting digital algorithms that enable segmentation to enrich computer programs.

Further this is not his first book to address segmentation. Seven years ago he produced a delightful book, at once droll but ever so instructive: *Strategic Segmentation and Target Marketing: How to Pick a Hotel.*

All of this coming out of a rich background that includes three college degrees, academic time at three universities, corporate duty with a Fortune 500 company, financial seasoning at two top Cleveland banks, creative work at a top 4A advertising agency, and, mainly, successfully operating his own financial and marketing consulting firm, North Union Associates.

I have been closely associated with him for twenty-five years. He and his company have performed a wide range of marketing tasks for us: participating in numerous focus groups, doing equally numerous surveys requiring detailed questionnaires and interviews, writing reports and guidelines . . . plus being my interface to academia and all the riches to be mined there.

This is all motivated by a desire to bring lifestyle segmentation concepts down out of the realm of theory into our workplace so that we may communicate better with readers and advertisers.

Hal Douthit, Chairman
Douthit Communications, Inc.
Sandusky, Ohio

Preface

Why this book? Why this book now? I wrote *How Consumers Pick a Hotel* in 1997, and many things have changed in American society since then: we have seen more immigration, we have seen a rise in Hispanic population born in the United States, baby boomers are about to start hitting sixty and are dealing with aging parents as people continue to live longer. And more and more changes have appeared, many of which will be discussed in the book. And *How Consumers Pick a Hotel* was written from a different perspective. As an aghast and upset reviewer at Amazon.com noted, the book was about consumer behavior and not how to run a hotel; it was a book designed to be read with a strategic perspective, as the subtitle *Strategic Segmentation and Target Marketing* stated. In many ways, much of this book is a revised edition of *How Consumers Pick a Hotel,* but in many other ways it is totally different and a different kind of book. Although not a cookbook, this book is less strategic in character and more focused on the here-and-now of segmentation.[1]

This book is organized in five sections. Sections I and II discuss segmentation theory as well as various methods of segmentation and then focus on "lifestyle" segmentation, which primarily means "psychographic" segmentation today. My clients and I have been heavily involved in various psychographic segmentation schemes and projects for almost a quarter of a century, from VALS and VALS 2 to PRIZM and a proprietary scheme; I will discuss all of these in detail. Sections III and IV explore some applications of lifestyle and psychographic segmentation based on personal experience, mostly with clients. Section V addresses some ways to communicate with the various segments that the firm has drawn or discovered and shares some thoughts about the future as the population (as well as the author) continues to age.

I wrote the book from July to September 2004. This is seven years after *How Consumers Pick a Hotel* was published, during which period I have not written anything for public consumption. As a consultant, I have periods of intense activity and periods of little or no activity with clients; the preceding seven years have been busy with client concerns—new services, new products, old products being revived and revised. All have left little or no time for writing or for the contemplation needed to be able to write. The intense activity slowed during the spring and summer of 2004; I started writing and have articles in review with various journals again. It was in pursuing getting one of the articles into review that I contacted Art Weinstein, who asked if I would like to submit a proposal for the current book.

So, the first debt I owe here is to Art Weinstein and the folks at The Haworth Press, who have once again shown their faith in an independent author. Although none of the books I have written has appeared on *The New York Times* best-seller list, sales must have been satisfactory. Furthermore, there are translations into Chinese, Spanish, and Indonesian either in print or underway; according to my daughter Abigail, I am now "incomprehensible in four languages"— an accomplishment indeed, considering that the only foreign language I ever studied was French! Of course, I have expressed my ongoing debt to my friend and client Hal Douthit by asking him to write a foreword to this book; my debts to Hal are ongoing and deep. A client who pays your bill is hardly rare; one who is a friend (and was a friend before being a client, but has continued being a friend during the almost quarter-century he has been a client) and allows a consultant to publish without consideration or wanting to see what is being written is, in my experience, almost unheard of. Hal has always encouraged me to write about him and his projects, never asking to see proofs before the articles or books appeared nor the finished works either; if what I have had to say was seriously negative, I have disguised the names. My family has always encouraged my writing, although Abigail is now at Colgate and not in the day-to-day orbit of the amount of time writing takes away from family—my son Teddy is still here, although he also spends time now with his mother. Various librarians, of course, must take credit for not sighing audibly at the umpteenth request for the same book to be retrieved because I need it again since I missed something the last time I had the book. And friends too numerous to mention, but some must be: Steve Verba, formerly of Realty One and Wyse Advertising, who reads almost every word I write (and frequently complains about many of them) and with whom I have co-authored; Jim Webb of Cleveland State and The American Real Estate Society, who has read much of the real estate work that shows up here and elsewhere and with whom I have co-authored several articles now in review; the folks at AdWriter, Inc., from Ed Toomey to Bryan Blue, who have worked on a day-to-day basis with the Tribes segmentation scheme and have offered me their experience with it. And last, but not least, Dr. Louise E. Hoffman of Penn State (Harrisburg), who has read every word I have written since I started writing again in 2004—and corrected most of them. Despite my friends and colleagues, I am sure there are mistakes in the book: *Mea culpa, mea culpa, mea maxima culpa.*

SECTION I:
NONLIFESTYLE ISSUES

Section I presents the theory of segmentation and other methods to segment other than on lifestyles. Much more detail about these can be found in *How Customers Pick a Hotel* (Cahill, 1997).

My son Teddy and I went to the Cleveland Auto Show in March 2006. I was not looking for a car (well, not really, but everyone is always looking at cars the way they look at houses—always with an interest), but I had to go for a client. Every major manufacturer was represented with a portion of the floor. In 2005, Teddy made fun of my first choice—the Subaru Baja, a very small four-passenger "pickup." I am driving a Toyota Corolla, the first sedan I have had since a 1964 Dodge. It is not easy having a small sedan; although the trunk is big enough, it is impossible to carry some items because there is no way to knock the seat down and put the hatch up. Pieces of plywood are $4' \times 8'$—much too long for a sedan. The Baja would take care of that problem. Teddy thought it was the dumbest car he had ever seen.

We walked the floor this year and picked out cars. I like the Dodge Caliber—a hatchback with lots of room, or possibly the Scion xB (Teddy's candidate now for the dumbest car ever, despite the fact that he is in the demographic and I am definitely not.) Age, lifestage, number of dependents—all these play into our product choices.

Chapter 1

Segmentation Theory

Segmentation, or market segmentation, is the dividing of a total market into its constituent parts by some method. Segmentation is not a new concept. It has been around for so long that a countervailing wisdom developed a couple of decades ago that for some products and some services the seller does not need to segment, that segmentation is too expensive of corporate resources to be worth doing and does not gain the firm anything.[1] In the past couple of generations, however, marketers have segmented their markets more often than not—Wilkie and Cohen (1977) discuss research dating from as far back as the mid-1950s. Despite a folkloric view of the 1950s as the golden age of mass marketing when everyone sat in a similar living room and watched *Leave It to Beaver* on identical television sets, there were, let us remember, *three* major U.S. car makers at the time, and not everyone used Tide to wash their clothes or brushed their teeth with Colgate toothpaste (I used Ipana). There were several competing products in many categories, and these products had what today we would recognize as differing brand personalities, attracting different kinds of customers; these product categories where, thus, segmented.

Art Weinstein (1987, p. 3) has called segmentation "the key to marketing success," a statement he reiterated in the revised edition (1994, p. 2), where he also discussed the "segmentation imperative." By 2004, Weinstein deals with the role that segmentation plays in business-to-business marketing, a subject I covered in *How Consumers Pick a Hotel*.[2] We are inundated with dozens of varieties of dozens of products and services that would not have existed until the product explosion of the 1990s, and in many cases those products would previously have been sold under different brand names. A huge literature has developed in the past couple of decades excoriating "brand extensions"—where a brand name is used on products that are different from the original. Coke becomes Coke and Diet Coke (which destroyed Tab as Coca Cola Inc.'s diet cola) and Cherry Coke and Vanilla Coke, etc. The reason that academic marketers condemn brand extensions is that the original product can get lost in the shuffle, and the "franchise" (now known as "brand equity" in discussions of the advisability of its appearing on the firm's balance sheet) built up over the years can be diluted or dissipated entirely. The case of Miller Lite is often pointed to as an instance of the dangers, because the extension became so successful that the extension almost destroyed the original brand—Miller Hi Life. Miller has made repeated, but rather desultory, efforts to resurrect Hi Life. Of course, another view of brand extensions is that the firm is simply expending some of the investment in the brand equity that has been built up over the years to build further equity. Given the high rates of new-product failure—it is typically stated that around 80 percent of new product ideas do not make it to their first anniversary in the marketplace—this may not be an unwise way to get new products to market with a hope of survival.

Segmentation can help in product and service development and marketing. Instead of Henry Ford developing the Model T for everyone, allowing variations in color as long as the variations were black, developing products and services for a specific segment allows for a much better focus on what people want and will pay for. This restatement of the Marketing Concept at the segment level—the Marketing Concept is a customer-oriented, integrated, profit-oriented philosophy of business, that can be bluntly stated as "Find out what people want and give it to them" (see Cahill, 1997, for an extensive discussion of the Marketing Concept)—shows a path for improvement in the new-product failure rate. This restatement of the Marketing Concept at the segment level is the foundation of segmentation as a strategy: either introduce one product to a specific segment as a solo target, recognizing that not everyone will buy the single product, or introduce an array of products with different features and benefits in each to attract several different types of consumers as multiple-target markets. It seems appropriate here to mention the Internet's use by consumers to search out new products and by producers to target customers. Despite major advances in Internet connectivity since I wrote about this subject in 1997, I still do not believe that the nature of the Marketing Concept has changed, nor has the definite increase in connectivity in the United States negated the need for producers to target one or more well-defined segments for their existing products or their new products, nor do I see this fact changing in the near future.

When undergraduate students are faced with the concept of segmentation for the first time, they usually decide that the basis for segmentation is by differences: what makes one group different from another must be what is important in segmenting. Such is not the case. What is much more important for the marketer is similarities: what makes the members of one group more like each other than they are like the members of another group. The use of similarities allows us, using one or more statistical techniques, to cluster people into groups and then to target our appeals to the members of one or more of the groups that our statistics have uncovered. Little work has been done on the theory of segmentation—it is a pragmatic, empirical technique driven by surface validity.

The segmentation scheme used must satisfy a number of criteria within the segments. Every segmentation scheme and its segments must possess the following criteria (DeSarbo and DeSarbo, 2003, pp. 473-474):

1. Differential behavior
2. Membership identification
3. Reachability
4. Feasibility
5. Profitability
6. Substantiality (Segments that are too small are apt to be artifacts of the method used.)
7. Responsiveness
8. Stability over time
9. Actionability
10. Projectability to the entire market

The schemes to be discussed in the rest of this book—whether syndicated, off-the-shelf varieties such as VALS 2 and PRIZM, or proprietary, such as Douthit Communications, Inc.'s Tribes—meet most if not all of the DeSarbo and DeSarbo criteria. It is possible that the substantiality test is the most difficult to achieve; very small segments may simply be the result of the segmentation methodology and cannot be eliminated. The Integrated group in VALS was only 1 percent of the population and could not be found by using the instrument that SRI used to place the population into the other eight VALS types. However, the theory that VALS was based on required that this segment be present in the population. On the other hand, it is just possible that there are such small segments occurring in the population. Obviously, a scheme with fifteen segments is more likely to have a very small segment than one that has only five.

Once the firm has decided to segment its market and has created the segments, it faces the problem of how to tell the segments that they exist and that the firm is interested in them. For some marketers, this is an easy task. Model railroaders, for instance, are not numerous; I doubt there are 2 million adults in the United States who are seriously involved with model trains. Nevertheless, there are two national magazines that specialize in reaching this general market—and nothing else. If one makes something for the serious model railroad market, one advertises in either *Model Railroader* or *Railroad Model Craftsman* and lets the editors of those magazines know about one's products. There are also a few other magazines that take this small segment one step further and specialize in one scale or in one type of railroading to model.

For other firms in other types of product or service markets, how to communicate with their customers is not as easy to determine. Despite the advocates of one-to-one marketing (Peppers and Rogers, 1993) and those who claim that the Internet has changed everything, we are still in an age when mass media, perhaps sliced a bit thinner than it was in the past, is the king of communications. Anyone who doubts that this is still true only needs to consider the brouhaha around the "wardrobe malfunction" at the 2004 Super Bowl halftime when Janet Jackson's breast was exposed for a few seconds—to somewhere around 143 million people, approximately 40 percent of the television sets in the United States. Try to get that level on the Internet. This fact of huge numbers is why television broadcasts still attract advertisers willing to spend money. It is easy—and quite cynical—to say, "How many of those 140 million are ever going to buy your product?" Without telling them it is available, the rejoinder is, none. The Super Bowl may not be the venue for going into much detail about a product or service, but it is a marvelous place to tell a lot of people a little about a product—especially a new product. It is up to the segmented communications plan to finish the job of reaching the potential buyers and showing them that the product is right for them.

Before considering specific kinds of segmentation schemes and approaches, where are we? There is always a temptation for a producer to attempt to make one product and get everyone to buy it as it comes. Production costs will be greatly reduced by following such a strategy, although selling costs may be higher. The problem is that this approach so rarely works, and it seems to work best in a tiny niche market that is so specialized as to be not worth the notice of many producers. There was no golden age of mass marketing in the 1950s (and probably not before). There were dozens of detergents offering different benefits, and television shows were broadcast on three different national networks with different appeals. Even in the 1950s there were three major U.S. automobile companies—General Motors, Ford, and Chrysler—offering Chevrolet, Pontiac, Oldsmobile, Buick, and Cadillac; Ford, Mercury, and Lincoln; and Plymouth, Dodge, DeSoto, and Chrysler models, respectively. Until the end of that decade, there were also Studebaker, American Motors, and Hudson Motors as well. All of the models were aimed at different people with different wants and needs—and finances. No "one size fits all," even in this most "marketed" of all products. Each car had a personality of its own to match that of a specific segment of consumers, and simply creating segments out of thin air does not work well. In a discussion of the statistical technique of conjoint analysis, a technique often used in segmentation analysis, Simmons and Esser (2003) state that conjoint analysis should be used to confirm or deny data validity because some attributes are either more or less important than expected, the needs of the segments are different from those hypothesized by management, and the segment sizes and demographic profiles do not match expectations—in other words, a priori hypotheses created by management need to be checked against the reality of the marketplace.

Segmentation schemes can be divided into two major groupings: those based on physical attributes (geographics, demographics, and the combination of the two—geodemographics) and those based on behavioral attributes of the customers (lifestyle, life stage, psychographics, and usage). The latter is the main focus of this book, of course.

REVIEW QUESTIONS

1. What is a brand extension? Why might market segmentation lead to brand extensions?
2. What is the Marketing Concept? What role does segmentation play in our understanding of the Marketing Concept?
3. How does segmentation make it easier to communicate with customers?

Chapter 2

Nonlifestyle Segmentation

Geographic segmentation is probably the oldest method for grouping markets. At its core is the assumption that people have different needs and wants because of where they live. The cliché about selling refrigerators to Eskimos is a recognition of the power of geographic segmentation (although Eskimos *do* use refrigerators to keep food from freezing in the cold). Because segments are created by grouping like with like, geographic segmentation makes sense: it is simple to understand, simple to perform and implement, and simple to manage. An example of geographic segmentation might be a chain of motels, with properties scattered from coast to coast, to the mountains and in urban areas. Some of the properties might be in Florida, where their prime season is between Thanksgiving and Easter; others might be in New England, with the prime season in summer. Given the geographic dispersal with the seasonal variations, the chain can no longer market all their properties as identical, even though they may be *physically* identical. Their different prime seasons dictate that fact. Simple geographic segmentation is often the best and least expensive method to deal with a market. The drawback to geographic segmentation is that it is not customer driven; rather, it is driven by the reality of the offering.

Demographic segmentation is probably the second-oldest consumer segmentation method. This is the old Bureau of the Census approach: designation by race, creed, color, sex, national origin, age, ability, and income. Demographic segmentation operates on the basis that people who have similar demographic characteristics operate similarly. Although the "truth" of this statement is obvious to anyone who has observed movies or television shows about teenagers, one must handle this type of segmentation very carefully on every variable.

Although it might be true that women do something differently from men, or teenagers from those in their sixties, in reality it is *most* women, or *many* teenagers, not all of them. Those teenagers who do something more like people in their sixties might not like to be reminded that they do not fit in with their peers—and those who do fit with their peers may resent the stereotyping. Probably the most famous demographic group—the Baby Boomer generation, born between 1946 and 1964—certainly has this difficulty. The Baby Boomer generation is really at least two different groups, split into "leading edge" and "trailing edge," having to do with whether they were of an age to be drafted and sent to Vietnam—or perhaps some other criterion, depending on the analyst. The focus on the Baby Boom generation is certainly nothing new; Yankelovich, Skelly & White/Clancy Shulman—a marketing-research firm—segmented Boomers into Self-Stylers, Materialists, and Nesters as early as 1987 (Brunton, 1987); even though Brunton thought three segments of such a large cohort was a bit oversimplified, it is at least as valid as "early" and "late," and it shows the difficulty inherent in segmenting—knowing when and where to stop. The age cohort that followed the Baby Boom, often called "Generation X" or "Gen X," was equally stereotyped in the popular imagination. It was the generation of "slackers," people who wanted to do little and succeeded. It was of the slacker generation that the statement of "why do you work four days a week?"—"cause I can't make enough in three" could be seen to be true. However, that age cohort will be starting to turn forty soon and is changing how many things are marketed—at least to them (Trachtenberg, 2004).

A demographic variable of interest is birth order. (However, I suspect that these variables can only be used as descriptive, because I know of no way to focus messages by birth order.) Claxton (1995) investigates the research done on birth order and concludes that, although it probably will never be a sole segmentation variable, birth order may be an important variable. Particularly given the Western trend to smaller families, there will be a larger percentage of first children and more only children; this may be more important for product and service planning than segmentation per se.

The truth of the danger of stereotyping that lurks within demographic segmentation schemes is made clearer when one remembers the continuing uproar over malt liquor, a beer product largely targeted at African-American consumers. Critics of advertising have complained for years that black faces were not present in advertisements in anything like their numbers in the population and when they are in advertisements, it tends to be for products aimed at blacks rather than for the general population; this criticism seems less true in the twenty-first century than it was in the past. Kaufman (1995) reminds us of these points as they apply to the physically disabled. Ferrell (1985) focuses our attention on the ethics of the advertisements written and produced to call the attention of our target market segment(s) to our offering.

Perhaps with women we reach the apex of the difficulty with demographic segmentation. Grey Advertising did a major survey (Beatty, 1995) and found that the "vast majority of women" surveyed said that "advertising is more unrealistic today than it was even two years ago"—80 percent said that the home life portrayed in ads is unrealistic versus 70 percent in 1993. Marketers were blamed for still "seeing women as one-dimensional." Too often, marketers see women as women rather than as people. Leeming and Tripp (1994) segment women as follows: Teens and young adults, Twentysomethings, Thirtysomethings, Late Boomers, Mature Market, African-American women, Hispanic women, Asian-American women, The Affluent, Working women, Homemakers, Mothers, and Singles. This is hardly helpful because of both the number of segments and their overlap: What does one do with an Affluent, Thirtysomething, Homemaking, African-American, Mother—to cite simply one example. Furthermore, because women so often do the shopping for the household—even for products that they themselves do not consume—there is the difficulty of dealing with the disconnect between user and buyer.

Nevertheless, demographic segmentation has great potential for targeting audiences at relatively low cost or difficulty and has the added bonus that it is focused not at the producer or product, but at something about the customer. Probably the demographic variable that most lends itself to credible, useful segmentation and targeting is age. Although not all teenagers are alike, any more than all women are alike, certain products and services can be offered to age groups that have higher propensities to consume them than other groups. There are, however, other variables that can work: height and weight, for instance; tall men's clothing stores are not new. Rarer are stores for short men, although stores for short and petite women are not new.

These segments are attractive for catalogue vendors, who all but define segmentation. Handled properly, with a great deal of discretion and understanding, any demographic variable is usable. The problem may lie in reaching the desired segment without offending either the desired segment or the segments not desired.

SECTION II:
LIFESTYLE ISSUES—
PRIZM, LOV, AND VALS

Section II provides examples of how we can deal with masses of people in other ways. We all live in neighborhoods surrounded by others. Are they like us or different? PRIZM states clearly that people live surrounded by people more like them than unlike.

Others sytems, such as VALS and LOV try to deal with people's innerness, their attitudes and values and what makes them tick. This approach requires more interpretation than simply check what a Zip Code neighborhood seems to be, but allows the marketer a rich understanding of the customer.

Chapter 3

Lifestyle Considerations

Unlike the "race, creed, and color" of demographic segmentation schemes, lifestyle segmentation is based on "activities, interests, and opinions," some of which reflect one's personality. This can be an attractive way for segmenting many product and service markets. It seems obvious to segment based on behavior and activities and interests; these are the parts of us that are observable by others and are less controversial than personal characteristics. Furthermore, it is now easy to communicate with the target segment or market today, given the vast number of special-interest media, including magazines and Web sites. It seems as though there is at least one magazine for any particular interest group, no matter how obscure or bizarre; remember the mention of model railroading above, with several magazines still being published in 2006.

However, there is some question about segmenting based on behavior and lifestyle. Lastovicka (1982) reviewed the literature to date and discovered that there was little published evidence to suggest that lifestyle-trait researchers had rigorously tested its validity, and, in fact, in the article his results only partially supported the validity of lifestyle segmentation. Bryant (1986) reviewed several practitioner-driven surveys that discovered lifestyle characteristics and traits that aided in delivering a more targeted message. Much of the difference in findings between these two seems to be the difference between the academic's outlook and that of the practitioner. Bryant (1986) claims that lifestyle segmentation research can be used to gain *insights* into consumer motivation, for turning on creative ideas, and as enrichment to demographic or geodemographic segmentation. She does not claim validity for the concept—only that it seems to work. Fennell et al. (2003) constructed a model and tested to see whether demographic or psychographic variables worked; they found that although these variables may predict *product* use, they did not predict use at the *brand* level. In the discussion of their findings, Fennell et al. (2003, pp. 241-242) stated that product use can be seen as a surrogate for the activities of our lives but that factors that explain brand preference (and, by extension, brand *use*) must reflect the substantive conditions that lead people to action. Because these factors arise from the intersection of individuals with their environment, they are probably undiscoverable for large enough groupings to use for segmentation purposes.

I believe that Douglas Holt holds the trump cards in this discussion (1995, 1997). Starting with his dissertation, he has examined the sociology of consumption. He concludes that using his method of analysis, one can unravel the social patterns of consumption according to categories such as class, gender, race or ethnicity, nationality, and generation in advanced capitalist countries in which "postmodern cultural conditions make tracing these patterns difficult with conventional approaches" (Holt, 1997, p. 326). Along the way he discards many of the stock methods of lifestyle analysis as being insufficiently nuanced; although theoretically and academically I believe that he is correct about the lack of nuance, for most market approaches to segmentation designed to sell more product or sell product more efficiently, the increase of nuance in his approach is unnecessary.

At some point we must come to grips with one of the problems with segmentation analysis: why are we doing it. If the goal is to carve the market up into smaller units in order to better focus our efforts on creating products for the smaller units that better suit their wants and needs and learn how to communicate with them directly—*in order to directly increase profits*—then on surface validity, doing it just because it works, is fine.

However, if our goal is to have a deeper, more measured understanding of our customers so that we can develop new products and services that fulfill their wants and needs so that we practice the marketing concept at a fairly deep level, then we need to deal with Holt's sociology of consumption and other similar work of a deeply academic nature. If we truly understand why our customers buy our products and use our services, what *deep* needs they are fulfilling, if we truly understand what makes our customers tick, we can design products and services to fulfill those needs—and keep our competitors out of our markets because they lack such understanding.

REVIEW QUESTIONS

1. List your demographic characteristics. Compare them to those of at least ten of your classmates and other students on campus. Does your list of colleagues seem to represent a coherent cohort, or is there significant diversity?
2. Which of your demographic characteristics seems the best one to use for segmentation purposes? Why?
3. How far from your permanent residence did you come to go to college? How far did the rest of your classmates? Think of your other college choices. Were they in the same area as you are now attending? Why or why not? From this exercise, would you say that colleges use geographic segmentation in their recruiting efforts?

Chapter 4

PRIZM

Geodemographic segmentation is based on the concept that birds of a feather flock together or, more correctly, that the birds in a flock are most likely similar to one another. That is, we are more similar to those who live around us than we are dissimilar, or as Weiss (1994, p. 9) states, "where we live affects our attitudes toward what we buy." I think that although this may be true, it reverses the direction of major causality; the statement should read, "What we think influences where we live."

Nevertheless, Weiss (1994) uses market mapping to highlight various consumer markets in the United States, usually in terms of markets that purchase an item well above or below the U.S. average. He then summarizes the markets. Of Cleveland, Ohio, where I live, he states, "Nothing about Cleveland truly stands out. With its average incomes, home values, and education levels, Ohio's largest city [it no longer is—it is now second largest in population] stays near the mean on consuming everything from books and stocks to motorcycles and pets" (Weiss, 1994, p. 119). However, Cleveland, like so many of the markets Weiss describes, is much too large to describe as a homogenous whole. Jonathan Robbin created PRIZM (Potential Rating Index for Zip Markets) on the basis that where people lived and who they lived among tells a lot about them. PRIZM is a system—originally of forty clusters—in which each Zip Code can be represented as belonging to a cluster that has a marketing and attitudinal personality of its own. This boils down to a "you are where you live" statement, but not in the sense that, say, all Clevelanders are alike. In fact, a Zip Code in Cleveland may have more in common with a Zip Code in San Diego than with other Zip Codes in Cleveland (Weiss, 1988).

As attractive as this concept is, with validity at first glance, it has some problems. First, despite the fact that the U.S. Postal Service

Lifestyle Market Segmentation
doi:10.1300/5560_06

provides the Zip Code for every address in the United States, I believe that PRIZM reverses cause and effect. Second, areas that Zip Codes cover are large. I live in 44120; half of this Zip Code is in the city of Cleveland, and the remainder is in Shaker Heights, a suburb. It comprises thousands of people of all races, religions, and economic standing, ranging from housing projects in Cleveland to some of the wealthiest people in Ohio—and a lot in between. The median house price in Cleveland is approximately $150,000 as I write this. The median house in the Shaker Heights part of 44120 has to be closer to $300,000; the median price in the Cleveland portion would be less than $150,000. I have seen analyses of this Zip Code done by PRIZM while testing the potential use of the system for a client; I knew enough about the Zip Code to be less than impressed with the results PRIZM produced. It is possible now to reduce the Zip Code to "carrier route" (Zip+4—the nine-digit Zip Code), reducing the size and population of the cluster; however, this simultaneously makes administration of the system more difficult. PRIZM bears a parentage in direct marketing and mail targeting; although it is attractive enough at first glance, until a system can come down to a manageable number of households, it seems too cumbersome to use for much beyond direct mail.

However, at targeting direct mail PRIZM can shine. One of my friends in the real estate business designed a marketing system for his firm and its agents. In addition to many components was a routine designed to find prospects every time an agent got a new listing. He had worked with PRIZM and knew its power in the right set of circumstances, so when he discovered that one of the factors in determining who might buy a house in Neighborhood A is where the other people in that neighborhood had moved from themselves, he designed a postcard routine to send to people in similar PRIZM neighborhoods to the neighborhoods that they had moved from. This routine was partly responsible for the firm's increase in market share of several percentage points. Table 4.1 shows PRIZM's new NE system, based on the 2000 U.S. Census. This system breaks the United States down into sixty-two segments clustered into fifteen groups.

Englis and Solomon (1995) tested the PRIZM segmentation scheme and found that one of the items that defines segmentation for most academics and practitioners—product choice and product use similarities among people—is possibly less defining than product *avoidance*.

TABLE 4.1. PRIZM'S NE segmentation group.

Group name	Segment
Group U1: Urban Uptown	Young Digerati
	Money and Brains
	Bohemian Mix
	The Cosmopolitans
	American Dreams
Group U2: Midtown Mix	Urban Achievers
	Close-In Couples
	Multi-Culti Mosaic
Group U3: Urban Cores	Urban Elders
	City Roots
	Big City Blues
	Low-Rise Living
Group S1: Elite Suburbs	Upper Crust
	Blue Blood Estates
	Movers & Shakers
	Winner's Circle
Group S2: The Affluentials	Executive Suites
	New Empty Nests
	Pools & Patios
	Beltway Boomers
	Kids and Cul-de-Sacs
	Home Sweet Home
Group S3: Middleburbs	Gray Power
	Young Influentials
	Suburban Sprawl
	Blue-Chip Blues
	Domestic Duos
Group S4: Inner Suburbs	New Beginnings
	Old Glories
	American Classics
	Suburban Pioneers
Group C1: 2nd City Society	Second City Elite
	Brite Lites Li'l City
	Upward Bound

TABLE 4.1 *(continued)*

Group name	Segment
Group C2: City Centers	Up-and-Comers
	Middleburg Managers
	White Picket Fences
	Boomtown Singles
	Sunset City Blues
Group C3: Micro-City Blues	City Startups
	Mobility Blues
	Park Bench Seniors
	Hometown Retired
	Family Thrifts
Group T1: Landed Gentry	Country Squires
	Big Fish, Small Pond
	God's Country
	Fast-Track Families
	Country Casuals
Group T2: Country Comfort	Greenbelt Sports
	Traditional Times
	New Homesteaders
	Big Sky Families
	Mayberry-ville
Group T3: Middle America	Simple Pleasures
	Red, White & Blues
	Heartlanders
	Blue Highways
	Kid Country, USA
	Shotguns & Pickups
Group T4: Rustic Living	Young & Rustic
	Golden Ponds
	Crossroad Villagers
	Old Millions
	Back Country Folks
	Bedrock America

Source: Claritas Corp.

We look to both positive reference groups, who might be in our own segment, and negative reference groups, who would not be. This is the dark side of segmentation: people mark who they are both ways.

If we are where we live, we certainly are *not* where we do not live (obviously) and quite possibly even more so. Although this statement may be colored by my having lived in Cleveland, which is split by the Cuyahoga River, and people who grew up on the East Side would never consider living on the West Side, and vice versa (in fact, jokes abound about needing shots and passports to cross the river even to go shopping), I think it is a generally valid statement. The first step we take in deciding where we will look for houses is determining whether we want to live "in or out," close to the city or away from it (American LIVES, 1991; Cahill and Polansky, 1997); it is as though buyers take a "helicopter shot" of the city. People who want to be close to the city are unlikely to buy a house out from the city, no matter how close a match it might be to the perfect house with other criteria they have, such as three-car garage or swimming pool. This statement of "in or out" trumps all else. If we are what we eat, then we are certainly *not* what we do not eat. And so forth. We are now back to the Holt (1995, 1997) sociology of consumption, in all of its deep nuance, with the Rook (1985) ritual consumption of goods and McCracken's (1986) cultural meaning of goods.

Part of this analysis may seem to apply more to the higher ticket items of houses and cars that we will be discussing later, with the highly charged item of food. We can all understand the roles of ritual and sociology as they apply to these items. But what about clothing? Oh . . . maybe we had better not touch that one. . . . What about lawn mowers? Hand or power? Electric or gas? Lawn service or do-it-yourself? All of a sudden, the yawning chasm of the role of sociology and ritual in consumption appears before us for almost any item, no matter how large and expensive or small and inexpensive. We are all assemblages of goods and services, it would seem.

REVIEW QUESTIONS

Log onto the Internet and go to www.claritas.com. At the area for testing a sample, obtain the PRIZM clustering for the Zip Code you live in. Answer the following questions:

1. Does the PRIZM description fit with your view of your neighborhood? Why or why not?
2. If the answer to Question 1 was no, which PRIZM clusters would you use? Why?
3. Do you think that people prefer to live with people who are like them or who are different?
4. If you were trying to market a pizza restaurant in your Zip Code, what approach would you use?

Chapter 5

Psychographics

Psychographics starts with a person's activities (what we do), interests (what we want), and opinions (what we think), often made into the acronym AIO. Psychographics has been around for a while; no one individual can claim to have created it, as it arose in the late 1960s and early 1970s from several strands of behavioral research. As a result of this creation from several strands of research, there are several directions in which psychographics go, some of which are mutually exclusive. It has been around for over a generation and uses lifestyle, social class, values, attitudes and other psychological attributes—often overlaid on some demographic information—to create multiple segments. At its heart, psychographics says that what people think and believe, the values they hold, and how they live and spend their money allow us to be able to predict consumer behavior (Demby, 1974, 1989).

To begin with AIO—which is generally a good place to start—one can come up with lists of activities that can describe a person or group of people: their work, their hobbies, what social events they attend, how they vacation, what they do for entertainment. For interests, of course the list starts for most people with family and goes through what and how they eat, what they wear, what media they read and watch. For opinions, most will list their opinion of themselves, what their stance on social issues is, their politics, what products they use. Out of all of this panoply of variables, one can create a profile that says a lot about an individual or group that shares these lists. Missing from this list, but added by many scholars and practitioners, is a direct statement of the values that an individual holds. There will be a discussion of the importance of values to psychographic segmentation later, in the discussion of VALS and the List of Values.

Lifestyle Market Segmentation
© 2006 by The Haworth Press, Inc. All rights reserved.
doi:10.1300/5560_07

Psychographics seeks to get to the "Who am I today" question and translate it into a group statement so that marketers can understand groups of customers and potential customers. None of us is rigidly unchanging from month to month, much less year to year. Our life trajectories take us through various changes in ourselves and our family and work circumstances. These changes mark us in ways that will change not only our inner selves but also what we buy and do not buy, what we want out of life, our interests, our activities, our opinions. My first post-MBA job was as Assistant Credit Manager of the Medusa Cement Company. Within a decade I had left that job and worked in the Employee Benefit Trust Departments of two different banks and finally started my own firm. During that time I also taught marketing at Cleveland State University. At the very least, my work clothing needs changed from sport coats to three-piece suits, back to sport coats. I had also changed as a person; my political opinions may have not changed, but during that decade I got married, traveled to France and Italy, read books, saw movies. I was irretrievably no longer the same person who had left Cleveland State with that MBA in 1975. How to market to *me* as I go through life? Or you?

Attitudes and values, plus demographics, therefore, yield psychographics. An attitude is an "enduring organization of several beliefs focused on a specific object." Values, on the other hand, "transcend specific objects and situations: values have to do with *modes of conduct and end-states of existence*" (Rokeach, 1968-1969, p. 550). Thus, a value is a type of belief central to one's belief system, about how one ought or ought not behave (Rokeach, 1968). The "ultimate function of human values is to provide us with a set of standards to guide us in all our efforts to satisfy our needs" (Rokeach, 1979, p. 48).

An individual's values and attitudes can and do change; values may be "enduring," but they are not immutable. They can change through creation, relatively sudden destruction, attenuation, extension, elaboration, specification, limitation, explication, consistency, and intensity (Williams, 1967, 1979); or acquisition, redistribution, rescaling of commitment, redeployment, and restandardization (Rescher, 1967). Moving away from "cherished personal positions and beloved hostilities may require a series of drastic events over time, recognition of a world beginning to crumble, or betrayal by those whose trust and understanding has affirmed one's personal investment in the cherished values (Sherif, 1980, p. 59). George C.

Wallace's repudiation of his lifelong segregationist posture and statements, along with an apology for being wrong, certainly fits within Sherif's framework.

The main feature of the value experience is that the experience is plural—we have "values." We frequently feel obliged to choose because our own values are often in irreconcilable conflict with each other; furthermore, we disagree with others about our values and theirs. Values are experienced in hierarchies or clusters (some values are more important or central to us than others). We experience our values as being "objective" and "natural," while those we oppose are "subjective" and "wrong" (Cadwallader, 1980). As Bellah et al. (1985) state, "'Values' turn out to be the incomprehensible, rationally indefensible thing that the individual chooses when he or she has thrown off the last vestige of external influence and reached pure, contentless freedom" (pp. 79-80). As we are going through the acrimonious presidential campaign of 2004 as I write, the "contentlessness" of values seems impossible—it is the very content of the value hierarchies and clusters that makes much of the acrimony possible.

An organization's or society's values can and do change as well, probably through the same processes as work within individuals. An example of a change that may be occurring with an organization is Scouting for All (see their Web site, www.ScoutingforAll.org, for details). Founded by a straight Boy Scout to counter the discrimination he saw in the Boy Scouts of America (BSA) against gay Boy Scouts, the organization has grown in strength and numbers as more and more Scouts and their families and leaders come to terms with the problems inherent in an organization that purports to teach boys how to become good men but that discriminates against boys and leaders who are gay—can gays not be "good" men? By whose definition? One of the taglines that BSA is currently using is that "America is returning to the values that Scouting never left." By this statement BSA means the Twelve Points of the Boy Scout Law, which do not include discrimination—and this fact confuses many boys who have been raised not to discriminate against others on any basis and who may have gay friends or relatives. The confusion is causing difficulties in recruitment for the Boy Scouts in many parts of the country and makes it more difficult to raise funds.

The controversy over gay Boy Scouts mirrors the intense controversy over various social values that has manifested itself at the beginning of the twenty-first century and surfaced in the Kerry-Bush presidential campaign. My values may not be yours; this fact should make it relatively easy to cluster people into different segments. Conservatives espouse one set of values, liberals another. With the use of the right signs, symbols, and words, one can easily appeal to conservatives and totally estrange liberals. Political campaigns and publicists do this sort of thing all the time and have done so for decades in the United States. Surely product and service marketers can do the same without the rancor and bitterness that political segmentation arouses. Lee and Hensel (1990) state that twenty years of research on values in consumer research has generated a lot of articles but little coherent result, and I doubt that they would change that opinion today. We all know values are important, but do not have a clear sense of how to use them (Prakash and Munson, 1985); it is clear that the profession has erred by not using a behavioral variable that is clear and useful. The fact that values may be difficult to define and may change (although Kamakura and Mazzon [1991] state that rank ordering of values has been stable in the United States over time) has probably scared marketers off. The most commonly used tool for values research has been the venerable Rokeach Value Survey, developed by Milton Rokeach several decades ago. He built two lists of values: eighteen "instrumental" values (those that we live by) and eighteen "terminal" values—desirable states of being (see Table 5.1). An individual facing the Value Survey places each set in rank order. Despite years of criticism (much of it of mostly academic interest), marketers have continued to use it because the potential results are too powerful to ignore.

TABLE 5.1. Rokeach's values.

Instrumental	Terminal
Ambitious	A comfortable life
Broadminded	An exciting life
Capable	A sense of accomplishment
Cheerful	A world of peace
Clean	A world of beauty
Courageous	Equality
Forgiving	Family security

Instrumental	Terminal
Helpful	Freedom
Honest	Happiness
Imaginative	Inner harmony
Independent	Mature love
Intellectual	National security
Logical	Pleasure
Loving	Salvation
Obedient	Self-respect
Polite	Social rooognition
Responsible	True friendship
Self-controlled	Wisdom

Source: Rokeach, 1973.

REVIEW QUESTIONS

1. List the magazines and other periodicals you subscribe to or read regularly. What does this list say about your activities and interests?
2. Compare your list in Question 1 with the lists of the others in the class. Are there similarities? Differences? What do these similarities and differences say about using Activities and Interests as segmentation variables?

Chapter 6

VALS and List of Values

Values have informed two different segmentation schemes in the past generation: VALS (and its second generation, VALS 2) and the List of Values (LOV) developed by Lynn R. Kahle (1983) out of frustration with the fact that Stanford Research was not releasing proprietary information about how the VALS segments were developed. Kahle went on to elaborate LOV extensively with several scholarly articles and books, frequently with co-authors.[1]

According to Arnold Mitchell (1983, p. 3), we are what we believe, what we dream, what we value. "For the most part, we try to mold our lives to make our beliefs and dreams come true." This belief and a lot of research led Mitchell and his colleagues at SRI to develop VALS in the late 1970s. VALS is at the intersection of Rokeach's work on values, Abraham Maslow's psychological hierarchy of needs, and the sociology of David Riesman et al. (1950/1961). The scheme, shown in every marketing textbook for thirty years, consisted of two parallel but unrelated streams of segments meeting in a single stem and combining in a single top. VALS is not a true psychographic segmentation scheme, as it combines psychographics and demographics into a vivid description of the nine types it recognized.

A major advantage that VALS had over most other psychographic schemes is the fact that it became so well known; a description of VALS made it into a mainstream journal (Atlas, 1984). Furthermore, it was a good description of the U.S. population. It has not been unusual for me to go to a meeting of managers, start discussing VALS, and have everyone nodding their head and saying "Yes, these are my customers." This is not to say that VALS was problem-free; it was far from that. The discrepancies in segment size (nationally, Belongers represented approximately 40 percent of the adult population while Emulators were only 10 percent) made it difficult for some marketers to deal with. Furthermore, the descriptions of some segments were decidedly negative (always a problem with segmentation schemes)—no one would want to be described as an "Emulator"—and the verbal description of those in the segment was no more flattering.

SRI recognized some of these problems and the additional problem that they felt that, although values were important for segmentation, the values they were then using were outdated and culture specific to the United States. In 1989, after several years of internal work, SRI introduced VALS 2. VALS 2 is more psychology driven rather than values driven, striving for universal meaning (Gates, 1989). Demographics is also downplayed, as VALS 2 is much more concerned with "what's going on in my customer's head" (Riche, 1989, p. 53); however, SRI added a resources component, recognizing that there may be gaps between consumer desires and the ability to fulfill those desires (VALS, 1989). Although many did not think that VALS was broken enough to need fixing (Winters, 1989—a sentiment with which I agreed), SRI responded to critics who felt that VALS was too theoretical and not predictive enough (Piirto, 1990). The VALS 2 segments are all between 8 and 17 percent of the population; furthermore, part of the segmentation is directly based on consumption in many categories. Despite using VALS extensively with clients and teaching it in many marketing classes, I have little direct experience with VALS 2 and do not know anyone else who has.

In an attempt to make values segmentation more academically respectable, Lynn Kahle and his fellow researchers developed another scheme, called the *List of Values* (LOV). According to Kahle, it surpasses VALS for four reasons. First—and most important to the academics—it is in the public domain. SRI has been strongly criticized for years for not releasing any information about the construction of its measure, even after the original VALS was superseded by VALS 2; academics always want to see metrics and measures so that they can replicate the research. Second, LOV collects demographic information separately from the values questions, unlike the VALS questionnaire, which combines the two. Third, the VALS questionnaire consisted of thirty-four questions; the LOV questionnaire consists of only nine. It is felt to be thus less obtrusive and that people would be less reluctant to complete it (although in my personal experience, long questionnaires are not necessarily prone to refuse, depending on the subject). Fourth, because the exact phrases from the survey instrument were retained in the studies using LOV (but not VALS), Kahle et al. (1986) have stated that communication of the research results to management is easier.

Kamakura and Novak (1992) looked at values segmentation again and concluded that the concept is a good idea, but the value *system* needs to be the variable used to segment, not just the top-ranked value as in LOV; thus, their conclusion is that any good values-based questionnaire is going to be a long one. In my experience Kahle's six-step process for using VALS (Kahle, 1983, p. 234) has little validity. He posits that one must create a survey, VALS classify the respondents, have an account executive at one's advertising agency interpret the classification results, weigh the client's desires as related to the foregoing interpretation, and have a *creative* person from the advertising agency render "these opinions" in an advertisement that is then directed back at the consumer. Kahle then states that "we have traveled a long distance from the potential consumer in the survey" mentioned at the beginning by the time we get to the end (Kahle, 1983, p. 234). I would agree with Kahle if what he said is what actually happens. What happens in my experience is that one creates a research instrument with the VALS typing instrument buried in it. No second step. Steps three and four go also, as in a very short time everyone at the client firm "speaks VALS" fluently—this is one of its true attractions. Regardless of its academic validity or lack thereof, VALS is self-explanatory after attending the SRI orientation, viewing the SRI videotapes, and reading some of the VALS reports that are available to subscribers. This reduces Kahle's six steps to two: making sure the "creative" at the agency understands VALS (not all agencies use VALS) and then reviewing the agency's work for VALS-correctness. Thus Kahle's four advantages of LOV over VALS really boil down to two: first, it is in the public domain and thus readily accessible to all researchers, and, second, it is shorter. Are these advantages worthwhile, particularly because there is no single database where the results of the LOV questionnaires used by researchers are stored? A good question.

REVIEW QUESTIONS

1. Rank order the two sets of values in Table 5.1 of the book. Compare your list of rankings with others in the class. Discuss the similarities and differences.
2. What does this ranking of values say about you? Is it reflected in the things you buy and use? How?

Chapter 7

Psychographics Again

How to develop a psychographic segmentation scheme? It is easier to buy one already developed, but let us assume that we want one that is proprietary, or at least specific to our product or service. Morgan and Levy (2002, p. 28) unequivocally state that the

> more specifically a segmentation study is focused on a [specific] product, service, or issue, the more actionable will be the segmentation strategy that results. Studies based on cohort analysis, general personality traits, lifestage, values, general psychographics, and lifestyle are inherently weak because they do not tie mature consumer segments to anything specific.

I completely disagree. A working lifetime of reading journal articles by academics doing segmentation study after segmentation study on specific products leaves me with the feeling that there has to be more; it is probably this overwhelming specificity that often leaves the reader hungry to know more about consumers than which brand of toothpaste will they buy, hoping to find some grand segmentation that will tell us something about consumers as people, not just as buyers of product after product after product. This has led me to prefer the grand approach, VALS or LOV or PRIZM, in an attempt to say *something*. One could be cynical and say that Morgan and Levy's statement that general segmentation schemes are worthless is driven by the fact that they collect fees for doing segmentation studies and would prefer to do them, one product/service/client at a time to increase their fee income. Also their repeated attacks on general segmentation schemes do tend me in that direction, for they attack every general scheme on the basis that it is general and thus does not say as much as one based on a specific product. Of course; I have never heard anyone say otherwise. However, one has to weigh practical considerations and say that perhaps after being VALS literate, for instance, one can predict which brand of toothpaste Belongers would be more likely to buy and that this is a good-enough statement for most practitioners.

Mitchell (1994a, b) provides a roadmap of the process of creating a roadmap to the process of creating a customized segmentation scheme. Mitchell (1994a) provides a technical discussion of the merits of factor analysis and cluster analysis, with a presentation of when to use which technique; Mitchell (1994b) presents multiple discriminant analysis in all of its technical complexity. He concludes, however, with a very nontechnical statement of the limitations of any or all of the statistical techniques mentioned: they all have reliability problems, which can be troublesome because the results of the analysis "frequently look plausible" (1994b, p. 16). However, operationalizing the segments by adding demographic data from the respondents can add to the robustness of the segmentation, adding a degree of reliability and replicability to the plausibility of the psychographic segments. (This is essentially what VALS and VALS 2 did, and this is why they are not strictly speaking psychographic segmentation schemes.)

Psychographics has been much maligned theoretically, usually by people grounded in statistics and psychological theory. Psychographics, according to these people, suffers from problems of the reliability and validity of the measures used. Merenski (1981) answers the critics directly with the statement that, for applied marketing purposes, the *usefulness of the measure is more important than its reliability or validity*. People's "behavior sets" are relatively coherent; if the psychographic profiles are drawn robustly, it is only at the margin that difficulty should arise—and these may be behaviors that have nothing whatever to do with marketing in general or with the specific product in particular. This is part and parcel of a debate that has been going on in marketing for a couple of decades about reliable, valid, and useless versus useful but "scientifically" shaky.

Wells (1975) succinctly states why psychographic profiles are useful, even in the absence of carefully constructed measures of reliability and validity: "consider the alternatives." The alternative is usually not a profile with carefully constructed measures; rather, it is a fallback position of crude demographics with someone's a priori statement of what "our customers" look like or tapes from a few focus group sessions. Also, those who market to these people, who design the packages and write the advertising copy, probably do not live the lifestyle of the typical customer. Wells continues, stating that psychographic segmentations are also useful:

> Marketers know that the customers for a product or service are frequently not much alike. They know that empirical segmentation procedures hold out the possibility of new insights into how consumers may be divided into groups. . . . Given [these dilemmas], many marketers have elected to conduct and use segmentation studies even when fully aware of the art's imperfections. (Wells, 1975, p. 208)

Little has changed in the thirty years since Wells's article, with the exception of there being less academic reluctance to accept psychographic segmentation—at least as descriptions of market segments, moving markets from numbers to flesh-and-blood people.

Psychographic segmentation schemes have been very popular in the academic press as well as the marketplace. Frequently reviled by nonusers as "flashy and unnecessary," one must be reminded from time to time about the purpose behind the use of psychographics. "[These] profiles were not designed to take the place of all other research tools. . . . Psychographic profiles should augment a total research and analysis package" (Wasson, 1987, p. 48). Wells (1975) made the same point in his review essay on psychographics and psychographic techniques; the procedure should be used to enrich the marketer's understanding of the people in the target markets. If we want to know the "how and why" of our customers, we will not be able to do so using strictly quantitative measures. The quantitative measures will only give us cold, hard, lifeless numbers and not tell us the "how and why" of our customers no matter how deeply we analyze them.

Psychographics is a tool. Like any tool, it has its limitations as well as its strengths. Townsend (1985) lists some commonsense guidelines for its effective use.

1. Use psychographics as one technique among many. (This is the point that Wasson [1987] made and is so practical that it should

not need to be repeated, but of course it needs to be reiterated constantly.)
2. Know how you will use psychographics before you start. (Of course! Do you need to tell people what your customers are like because you don't know any? Or are you trying to accurately design a product for a particular segment? Reliability and validity issues may matter in the latter case, but probably not in the former.)
3. Never stop monitoring the market. (This is true whether we are talking segmentation or selling!)

Piirto (1991) delineates eleven lessons for avoiding the pitfalls of psychographics, most of which have general applicability for most segmentation schemes—or much of marketing itself.

1. Know where you've been.
2. Extract the best from both quantitative and qualitative research.
3. Understand the underlying consumer trends.
4. Weigh the relative value of using a syndicated broad-based scheme (such as VALS).
5. Use whatever techniques you are comfortable with to get the profiles of all potential customers.
6. Identify the underlying motivators.
7. When entering large foreign markets, market to the similarities, but make sure you understand and never underestimate the differences.
8. Understand the uniqueness of each local or regional market.
9. Carefully consider the sample size.
10. Make the ultimate goal of your research to identify product-specific attitudes and behaviors.
11. Know everything you can about your core customers.

I would add a twelfth lesson here, particularly true for psychographic segmentation, but true in general for all segmentation schemes. Keep testing, keep researching, keep measuring. People change, trends change, values change, everything changes. The truth of this statement has been brought home recently by the release of the 9/11 Commission's Report and the constant reiteration that the events of September 11, 2001, have changed everything in America. We as a people certainly seem willing to reorder our priorities in the face of those events; I am less sure whether our underlying values have changed, but the possibility remains that they have. Such re-ordering of priorities and changing values has major implications for marketers. If you as a marketer set your psychographics in stone in Year One, even without a major event such as September 11, 2001, by Year Six, the percentages of each segment may be radically different from what your model predicted, your media spending will be misdirected, your packaging and manufacturing will all be off, and you will not have a clue as to why things are not working. Wells and Moore (1989) state that "our experiences . . . of periodic measurement have shown us time and again that periodic measurement allows us to separate the obvious truths that are true from the obvious truths that are not true." Keep testing, keep researching, keep measuring. You need to know who your market is, not just how much you are selling, which is why scanner data, touted as a panacea of information not so long ago, are insufficient. Although scanner data with the addition of customer-number information (such as a supermarket or drugstore "frequent shopper membership card") can give you both.

Behavioral segmentation derives from the hypothesis that past behavior is a good indication of future behavior. For instance, those who have bought Colgate toothpaste in the past are more likely to buy Colgate in the future than those who have not, and they are more likely to buy Colgate than they are to buy Crest (assuming, of course, that they have been satisfied with Colgate). Thus, it seems easy to segment based on behavior; "heavy users, light users, and nonusers" have been the segments most often hypothesized in marketing textbooks for decades. Communication to the different segments might prove difficult, as media habits, income, and other factors may be very similar among the three segments. The airlines' "frequent-flyer" programs, often touted as "loyalty marketing," are really reward systems for repeat purchase behavior and not really "loyalty" systems in any commonsense use of the word "loyalty"; they do not separate heavy users from light users, because anyone can join most of the programs.

Part of the reason for the marketers' emphasis on past behavior is the fact that academic marketers have had a persistent problem: attitudes research has been largely qualitative rather than quantitative and focused in strange directions. This has led to dissatisfaction with the field and to marketers' attempts to change attitudes. "Rather than change attitudes, [integrated marketing communications] seeks to change behavior. . . . We have never really been able to link attitudes to behavior" (Schultz, 1994, p. 44). The only problem with this statement is that it is one of the Wells and More's "obvious truths that are not true." It is true that psychologists and other behavioral scientists have had difficulties linking attitudes to behavior in laboratory settings and that marketers have tried to deal with "Attitude Toward the Ad"—whether a positive attitude leads toward purchase of the brand.[1] However, those who work with people in a social-service setting—ministers, social workers, doctors, etc.—know better. William G. Holliday, formerly the Senior Minister of Plymouth Church of Shaker Heights, stated this fact bluntly in a sermon in 1993: "Not only are attitudes cultivated by people; people are cultivated by attitudes, particularly when they have developed into habits." Habits are, of course, a specific form of behavior, one where we act without further conscious thought. At the very least, attitudes represent a portion of behavior—"percentage of variance explained," to put it at its statistics worst. Attitudes form predisposing and/or precipitating factors for action (Camacho and Schmalensee, 1989).

Sherif (1980, pp. 18-19) pointedly said that an "attitude is inferred from behaviors (verbal or nonverbal), without which we can never know whether a persona has an attitude." Attitudes are not static psychological entities that can be separated from the flow of action, but rather are integral parts of action. Attitude and action are linked in a continuously looping and reciprocal process, "each generating the other in an endless chain" (Kelman, 1980, p. 135). Kelman feels that there is *no* significant attitude change possible without action—overt behavior that "produces some change in the environment and has real-life consequences for the actor" (Kelman, 1980, p. 119). Buying and using a product will change one's attitude toward that product and its competitors, as well as toward the problem that that product is supposed to solve. And so on. Perhaps these attitude changes will, subtly and only at the margin, shift one into another psychographic segment.

There is a further point to adopting segmentation schemes: it allows a firm to manage its language and its culture (Susbauer et al., 1994). When a firm adopts a segmentation scheme, it becomes an argot within that firm in relatively short order. In my experiences with clients, within a few months of adopting VALS, everyone at the company was competent in "VALS-speak." Anyone could say, "Oh, he's a Belonger" or "she's a Soc Con" correctly, and everyone else would know what that person meant. In a multidivision company, or in one with far-flung operations, this is no small benefit. For reasons that are not germane here, the client I am discussing was unable to fully utilize VALS in its products nor in its marketing efforts for those products. Most of the firm's customers did not know that the firm was a VALS subscriber, and they were not advised how to use VALS in *their* marketing effort, which, because the client's products were not sold to end customers, would have been a benefit to both the client and its customers. VALS was never adequately utilized to derive a competitive edge for the firm. However, being a VALS subscriber enabled this highly fragmented and geographically dispersed firm to communicate internally in the same language about customers.

There is a large literature about organizational culture and how to change it—and, in fact, whether it can be changed. Language is a part of culture; the internal language that an organization uses (and every organization has its own argot) is a part of organizational culture. Language is at the crux of the organizational culture that can be changed; change the language and the culture *has* to change (Wilkins and Dyer, 1988), although one cannot say ahead of time just how that culture will change. Adopting VALS made the organization think about its customers a certain way; adopting PRIZM would have made the same firm think about its customers in a different way. Both ways would be correct, because the segmentation schemes are, by definition, internally coherent and consistent. However, the firm would be different if it had adopted PRIZM instead of VALS.

REVIEW QUESTIONS

1. Psychographics is frequently maligned because of reliability and validity issues. Define reliability and validity in this context. Do these issues matter? Why?
2. Psychographics has been defended because it is useful. Does usefulness matter more than reliability and/or validity to a marketer? Why or why not?

3. What is "brand loyalty," and why is it important for segmentation? Is this still a valid construct in an age when loyalty supposedly no longer matters? Why or why not?
4. Describe an instance when a change in one of your attitudes toward something was caused by rubbing against a differing reality. Was the change permanent?

SECTION III:
LIFESTYLE TARGETS

Each of the chapters in Section III represents a different lifestyle market and how to approach it. Matures (not "old folks" anymore), Teens and Tweens, Ethnics, and the disabled might all seem to be nonlifestyle, demographic groups—and, in fact, are part of the usual demographic litany.

Nevertheless, marketing to these groups in a lifestyle fashion works better, provides a richer, deeper understanding of the people in the markets. Matures (however one wants to define this group) actually represents many age segments. But it also represents many different lifestyles. People fifty-five to sixty (to take a group—not at random . . . it is mine) are frequently still working full time and thus may have more in common with those people forty-five to fifty than seventy-five to eighty, but may also be looking ahead to their time in the latter age group—and may still have parents alive in the seventy-five to eighty-five age cohort and be responsible for their purchases of health care or food. Demographic segmentation alone would not catch this fact, but dealing with lifestyles would.

Chapter 8

The Mature Market

The "Gray" market, or "matures," or "seniors," or by whatever name it goes by, is a big market. There were 78 million Americans aged fifty years and older in 2001 (approximately one-third of the total population); they control 67 percent of U.S. wealth. Furthermore, households headed by someone in the fifty-five-to-sixty-four year age group had a median net worth of $112,000 in 2000—fifteen times the median net worth of the under-thirty-five age group. This is clearly a market worth exploring, even if your product or service *seems* to be an unlikely match for this demographic segment (Greene, 2004). Of course, there is always the problem of marketing to this market without totally turning off younger buyers, but the numbers make it imperative to most companies to start spending money to attract the attention of older consumers. There is always pressure to attract younger consumers; some of that pressure is a residuum of the fact that the Baby Boomer cohort was so huge—and young in the 1960s, 1970s, and 1980s. They no longer are young. Some of the pressure is simply the ongoing effort of people in advertising and "creative" areas to be cool and hip. This pressure needs to be fought tooth and nail by any firm that wants part of the mature market.

There is always a problem that the people in the advertising industry are not in the same segments as the consumers of the products they produce advertising for, and this is particularly true of age. Advertising has long been an industry of the young; advertising aimed at older people has often carried the condescending and patronizing images of youth looking into the distance and not wanting to see themselves in a few decades or refusing to face the fact that they are writing messages for their parents or their grandparents and not to the people who will buy the products. This is not solely an American problem or a twenty-first-century problem, as Dorothy Sayers's *Murder Must*

Lifestyle Market Segmentation
© 2006 by The Haworth Press, Inc. All rights reserved.
doi:10.1300/5560_11

Advertise—the story of a 1920s English advertising agency—shows (Sayers, 1933).

We as a society still carry many stereotypes of older people; when we think "mature" or "old," we are thinking mostly of people in their eighties and nineties, grandparents perhaps near the ends of their lives, frail, white-haired, stooped, slow in mind and body. There are plenty of older people who fit that stereotype. The recent dedication of the World War II Monument in Washington, DC, brought them out; but World War II veterans in 2004 are at least in their late seventies. Is this the only segment of older people? If so, then those in the advertising agencies who make fun of the "Metamucil for lunch and Geritol for dinner" segment might be right.

However, there are other ways of viewing older people. As the Baby Boom generation ages, expect to see the number of affluent households in the fifty-five-to-seventy-four-year-old age group surge. By 2008, the number of households headed by people ages fifty-five to seventy-four will grow about 15 percent to over 30 million; households in that age group with an annual income of at least $100,000 (in 2002 dollars) will grow 60 percent to 6 million. Affluent households also frequently have substantial assets; households headed by someone aged fifty-five to seventy-four with and income of $100,000 have net worth over $1.5 million (Francese, 2001, 2002). This is clearly not Aunt Mary sitting alone in the nursing home on Medicaid. This growth in income and assets in the younger mature market is likely to fuel major changes in buying and marketing: luxury travel, luxury cars (but, because we are talking about Boomers and not their parents, not the big American boats of the past), more restaurant meals— as long as good health lasts, this segment of the mature market is likely to spend in ways that their parents did not, but at the luxury end of the way they spent when they were younger. There will still be a Lexus, not an Oldsmobile, in the driveway.

Much of the difference between the Baby Boom generation and the cohort before it comes from a higher degree of education; 28 percent of women born from 1946 to 1954 are college graduates versus 19 percent of those born between 1936 and 1945. More of the Boomer women work full time (two-thirds versus one-half) and earn an average of $50,000 per year themselves. It is this second statistic that probably drives the affluence of the Baby Boom generation; many in this generation have two wage earners in the household, and, although they have saved less than the previous generations and thus have to continue to earn later in life, their incomes have fueled luxury and near-luxury consumption (Francese, 2001), and better health will allow them to continue working later in life.

Walker (2002, p. 9) divides the Mature market (which he calls "seniors") into four groups as follows:

Age Group	Stage of Life
55-64	Preretiree and early retiree
65-74	Retiree
75-84	Older retiree or mature adult
85 and above	Elderly

I fit into Walker's "seniors" as a preretiree, but I certainly do not *feel* like a "senior." I am not a member of AARP, and I am not sure that marketing to the fifty-five-to-sixty-four age group as "seniors" or part of the "Mature market" is going to make points with large numbers of us in this demographic. However, we are clearly *not* Gen X.

In an article written in 2002, Robert Snyder stated that the key to capturing the mature market is to understand the essential values and convictions of the sixty-two-plus crowd (his definition of "mature"). His employer, J. Walter Thompson, has divided the mature market into eight segments based on the importance those in each group assign to different values: True Blue Believers, Hearth and Homemakers, Fiscal Conservatives, Woeful Worriers, Intense Individualists, Liberal Loners, In-Charge Intellectuals, and Active Achievers (Snyder, 2002, p. 49). Except for age, the segments that Snyder talks about are probably fairly well represented in the nonmature population, albeit in differing proportions; remember that our values can change over time, but that may only be in their rank order. Snyder states that True Blue Believers and Hearth and Homemakers represent 40 percent of the mature population and represent the "stereotypical" values of the mature population (although I would think that the Fiscal Conservatives and Woeful Worriers are also included in the list of stereotypes many of us carry around when talking about "Matures"). Francese's (2002) article helps offset this emphasis on our stereotypes of older Americans. Although it is true that as we age we need more health care services and products, Francese accurately points out that what constitutes that health care is changing as the affluent fifty-five-to-seventy-four-year-olds (who are already spending $70 billion of their own money on health care—in addition to money from insurers, employers, and the government—according to government statistics) avail themselves of cosmetic treatments, or spa treatments, or other items that we normally do not associate with older people. Furthermore, if the wealthy are spending $1,000 or $2,000 a day at a spa, there will probably also be a market for a more down-market version of the same services as the less wealthy discover that they want some of the same services.

One of the difficulties with the "mature" market, which should be apparent from the previous discussion, is the lack of consistency among the definitions of what constitutes "mature." In the previous generation, it was relatively easy to define. Most large firms had retirement ages of sixty-five; Social Security did likewise, but it allowed for early retirement at a reduced benefit at age sixty-two. Sixty-five became the gold standard of the Mature Market—those sixty-five and older (or in rarer cases sixty-two), large numbers of whom were retired and no longer working even part-time for pay. Thus, the definition had both a demographic component—age—and a behavioral one—retirement; and the definition was well-understood in both components.

Today it is much more complicated. Many large firms have abandoned defined-benefit retirement plans for defined-contribution plans, which allow for much greater flexibility in retirement (and if one's investments in the plan have done well, a large monthly benefit). On the other hand, many people are not retiring at age sixty-two or sixty-five; whether for financial reasons (college expenses for their children, house payments that continue far into the future because of refinancing or whatever) or for personal reasons, many continue to work well past "normal" retirement age—sometimes for their old employer sometimes not, preferring instead to take advantage of "retirement" from the rat race to obtain a more "fulfilling" job.

Thus "mature" has become solely a demographic as more and more people in this age cohort continue to work. If they are working, then long, leisurely vacations may not be an attractive service—and neither would many other "traditional" goods and services that appealed to their parents.

REVIEW QUESTIONS

1. Find the demographic information for at least ten "matures" in or around the college community you used for Question 1 in Chapter 2. Compare and contrast them with yours.
2. Make a list of goods and services you use on a frequent basis: entertainment, food, etc. Get a list from the same people you used in Question 1 above. Compare and contrast the lists.
3. Make the same list for your parents and, if they are still alive, for your grandparents.
4. Compare and contrast the lists for the three questions above. Compare and contrast the lists with those of your classmates.
5. Based on the four questions above, would you say that there is a coherent "mature" market, or are there different markets for people of different ages, even when they are all fifty-five or older?

Chapter 9

Teens and Tweens

Who are "tweens"? The glib definition is those too old for elementary school but too young to get into a PG-13 movie on their own. Siegel et al. (2001, p. 27) define them as children between eight and twelve years inclusive (although eight seems awfully young to me—starting this young almost begs to have "early tweens" and "late tweens" because anyone who has been a parent can tell you there are significant differences between the two ages). Siegel et al. state that this group is different in cognitive, social, and physical development from those both younger and older. They further contend (2001, p. 29) that this age group is a significant segment, representing (in 1999) 19.5 million people, larger than the Asian population in the United States. In make-up, it is 66 percent white, 15 percent African American, 15 percent Hispanic American, and 4 percent Asian American.

Size alone does not make a segment worth trying to reach; remember the DeSarbo and Desarbo (2003) list in Chapter 1. Substantiality is only *one* criterion among their ten. The segment must spend money and spend it in ways that are different from other segments. Siegel et al. (2001) claim that not only are tweens possessed of significant amounts of spending money—in allowances and gifts and in earnings from babysitting, lawn mowing, paper routes, and other sources—but they also heavily influence spending by their parents in certain areas: food (both away from home and at home), clothing and shoes, and toys. Some of this influence is positive; some is what they call the "nag factor" (others would not so dignify it, but would call it the "whine factor"). These considerations would lead me to state that the true Tween market segment is middle-school-aged kids (most are ages eleven to thirteen or fourteen); much younger than eleven and their access to money is limited mostly to allowances and gifts. It is middle-schoolers who provide much of the babysitting, pet-sitting, lawn-mowing, and paper-delivery (at least that of the neighborhood weekly since the urban dailies have sold out to adult carriers) labor in most neighborhoods, and they *do* spend money. B*tween Productions, Inc., has launched the Beacon Street Girls brand of books sold either separately or with pillows, jewelry, and small duffle bags; the expectation of the CEO of B*tween Productions is for sales of $1.5 million the first year and $50 million in revenue by year five (Archambeault, 2004). Although much of the marketing emphasis continues to be on tween girls, the boys in this segment also have money and spend it, too—differently from their older or younger brothers (Halpern, 2004). Now even Barbie, the doyen of the tween market, has gotten into the act. Mattel has been working to increase interest and make her "more relevant to modern eight- to twelve-year-olds" (Sook Kim and Vranica, 2004, p. B1). Mattel has developed a new line of clothing and a perfume to capture tweens' attention. They have developed a television commercial with actress and singer Hilary Duff; also, tween girls wearing furry pink vests and preppy plaid miniskirts upstage Barbie herself, who appears for only a brief moment in the ad. Sook Kim and Vranica report that analysts are puzzled by the firm's attempt to ignore dolls for tweens and aim at fashion. Furthermore, with schools cracking down on clothing that shocks the elders and enforcing more restrictive dress codes, the way for tweens to express "cool" may now be in school supplies and other accessories, including backpacks, electric scooters, and three-ring binders (Lipton, 2004).

American Greetings Corp. has released a line of toys, scented stationery, stickers, journals, and gadgets aimed at six-to-twelve-year-olds that lets them communicate with friends and "show off their creativity" (Cho, 2004). No one has ever targeted this age group in quite this manner. According to Jeffrey Conrad, the creative director for the product line (issued in conjunction with Nickelodeon Television), the "first time anyone really uses social expression products is when you give kiddie valentines, and until you're a grown adult, you pretty much don't use them again" (Cho, 2004, p. C3). Condescension from marketers is certainly not the exclusive purview of those who sell into the Mature market.

Conrad is not correct about the fact that there is nothing between "kiddie Valentines" and adult expression products: many teenaged girls use lots of "social expression products"—greeting cards. In the mid-1990s, I worked at Wyse Advertising in strategic planning. One of the my clients was American Greetings' Creata-Card division, which at that time dealt with touchscreen kiosks that created self-designed and printed greeting cards. My department was asked to prepare and present a SWOT analysis of Creata-Card. I did a tremendous amount of research into greeting cards and their markets and marketing. One of the reasons I was hired at Wyse was that I had worked with a client who dealt with touchscreen kiosks for real estate.[1] At that pre–World Wide Web time, computer kiosks were uncommon but not rare, and they seemed to be the wave of the future for delivering information and paper items: in addition to greeting cards, there were kiosks dispensing theater tickets, insurance policies, and other items. They definitely attracted a more youthful user than other media and channels.

Greeting cards, on the other hand, were bought in large numbers by older women. In fact, as I recall the statistic, the "heavy greeting card user" was a woman in her sixties and sent five or more cards per month—not including Christmas cards. She bought her cards in bulk, often in boxes of mixed types: birthday, sympathy, anniversary all in the same box, usually with sentimental verses and with muted graphic images. Creata-Card, on the other hand, had snappy sayings (for those cards that the user didn't create the verse at the machine) with extremely bright graphics. When my kids and I went to use one of the machines to make their mother a Mother's Day card so that I would have experience with the machine before the presentation to American Greetings, we immediately ran into difficulties. Their printer had no paper, so printing out the card was going to be impossible. The screen was too high for my then six- and ten-year-olds to see, much less use.[2]

Armed with all the research and discussions with other people at Wyse, I was ready to present to American Greetings and to point out to management that their target audience of mature women was not the market that was currently using Creata-Card and that there were difficulties with using the machine and with the cost (at that point, Creata-Cards were $3.95 each; boxed cards were about that much for twenty-five to thirty, depending on assortment and store pricing). The market that was currently using Creata-Card were teenaged girls, who would send ten to twelve a year; they would stand around the machine in a group and help each other make the card as a social event. I was told, in no uncertain terms by American Greetings' management, that this was *not* who they wanted to attract, that, in fact, they wanted help in discouraging this group from using the machine because their presence was driving the older women away. They wanted our help in driving their users away and getting *their* ideal target market to use the machine.

Very short sighted? Of course. Did it work? No. I was reminded on the spot, and told management the story, of an incident with Info-Vision. They had installed a kiosk that showed houses for sale in a mall outside Denver, Colorado. The mall manager noticed that young boys would start playing with it. Because houses for sale are not inherently interesting to that age group—nothing on the machine would let them zap or shoot the houses or gobble them up or to play any other arcade-game activity—they would leave, but after a short time they would return with their father in tow. Real estate agents will kill to get the male involved in the search process; here seemed to be a way for this to happen. Driving the young boys away because they were not the demographic in which the real estate agent was interested would have been short sighted, and I have always thought that American Greetings mishandled Creata-Card because its target market was incorrect given what Creata-Card was. It of course evolved into the electronic greeting card, typified in its early days by Blue Mountain Company, an early Web-based success story, a company with almost no revenue that was bought by Excite.com for almost $1 billion—and later sold to American Greetings for a mere fraction of that price as Excite.com desperately tried to recover from a string of disasters during the dot-com downward spiral of the 1990s. Teenaged girls were sending hundreds of electronic greeting cards to each other—for free—and they continue to do so, with such greeting cards offered at hundreds of sites ranging from Yahoo.com through AmericanGreetings.com to Care2.com (for the environmentally conscious). Some of the differences in greeting-card purchasing are generational, but some of the generational differences are seen as a moral divide, particularly by those on the side of the heavier users of paper cards. Cards are seen as an index of the time and effort put forth in a relationship (and the monetary expenditure is weighed in as well), and the looking for and purchase of a paper card takes longer than creating and sending an electronic one, thus endowing the relationship that justifies a paper card as being "worth more" than one that "only" justifies an electronic card—to the older buyer of paper cards (West, 2002).

I found a way out of American Greetings' dilemma. Because their own research showed that about two-thirds of the Creata-Cards were hand delivered in person rather than mailed, I felt that raising the price of the card (to perhaps a range of around $10 per card) and framing the card as a gift would work. "Here is this card that I made for you" would take the card out of the category of a thirty-five-cent boxed card into a self-created, hand-crafted item that *I* make for *you*. I can make the "I'm sorry I broke your lamp" card, the "Congratulations on winning the Science Fair" card—those cards that no one will make on a mass basis. Although there was some feeling at Wyse that this might be a valid approach, no one could remember an instance when a product's manufacturer changed categories for an existing product (to be fair, neither could I); the idea was never presented to American Greetings.

The teen market is a fast-changing market at the best of times and becomes hyperfrenetic upon occasion. Teens are dealing with rapid social, cultural, and structural changes as a routine part of their normal lives; a primary method by which they deal with this situation is to adopt various consumer lifestyles through which their fluid identities can be constructed. Their lifestyles seem to be concerned with the continuity of change (Miles, 2002). In nonjargon terms, they dress and act in ways that seem deliberately intended to upset their elders. Within a decade, Abercrombie & Fitch Clothiers went from providing fashion statements for college students to providing fashion for their younger siblings in high school and then for the tweens in middle school. Within that time span, of course, as the younger market adopted the brand, A & F lost the older market because the company was no longer "cool" for them. The only constant for A & F was its adherence to its "edgy" catalog, often considered borderline soft porn. As long as its target market was the over-eighteen college students, this mattered little; once their average shopper was a middle-school tween, A & F had difficulty with its catalog look. Wet Seal, a hot Teen marketer in the 1990s with its low-rise pants and cropped tops, missed the turn to the preppier look in the early 2000s and had to bring in teen "stylizers" to punch up the current look and get their friends back into the stores (Kang, 2004).

Furthermore, there is another teen market that is important: the teen shopper who is the regular or semiregular shopper for the family now that a large number of adult women are in the labor force. If the wife of a husband-wife dyad is working forty hours a week as her husband does, someone needs to do the grocery shopping and the drug-store shopping and to run other consumption errands, even if it is not the "normal" weekly shopping but rather a more-sporadic, episodic kind. The person doing this shopping is usually an older teen (driver's license needed!) and usually female. Although the products and brands may be specified by the adults (particularly if the teen is not one of the consumers of the item), often they will not be; advertisers became aware of this situation many years ago and reacted by advertising in the usual teen media for products that would not normally be seen as something appropriate to advertise there (Malcolm, 1987). Now, almost twenty years later, this trend has continued.

These segments make up what has been called Generation Y—the 70 million children of the Baby Boomer generation. Generation Y comes in three waves (Paul, 2001). The first are those born from 1977 to 1983 and represent slightly more than one-third of the cohort. Unlike their older counterparts—the notorious Generation X—these young adults are optimistic about their earning power; they tend to spend heavily even while in college. Although they are more computer literate than their parents, they came late to the Internet and wireless communications. The second wave, those born from 1984 to 1989, also represent slightly more than one-third of the cohort. They also spend—on average $4,000 per year, of which $3,000 is "their own money," and a major proportion of that spending goes toward clothing, even for boys.[3] They also have long-term goals; almost one-fifth of this group owns stocks or bonds. The third wave, those born from 1990 to 1994, represent nearly one-third of the cohort. Although they are seemingly very young, they spend a lot—partly because they receive substantial cash gifts, mostly from their grandparents. In addition, this group wields a disproportionate influence on the family spending, often with the blessing of their parents who trust their knowledge and information-gathering ability.

How to reach the Teen and Tween markets? There are the traditional media outlets: television shows aimed at them, magazines such as *Seventeen, YM,* and the fan magazines, radio stations that play music aimed at them. These are fast-moving and fragmented groups, however, whose demographic composition dictates that significant portions of the age group disappear at the upper ends and appear at the lower ends each year. A lot of effort and attention are currently being devoted to product placement rather than to media advertisement. Cell phone manufacturers are trying to get their phones featured in movies, the Ford Focus automobile was one of the prizes on the popular TV show *American Idol,* Coca-Cola had its logo featured on the same show very prominently behind each of the judges, and there are now products being placed in video games, appealing as strongly there to the Tween market as to the teens (Harper, 2004). Product placement is a method extensively used in all segments to reach people now that it is "impossible" to reach them on broadcast or traditional print media because "no one" views these media.[4] Another method of reaching these markets (and others) is to place linked advertisements on Web search engine sites such as Google. Google's AdSense program offers advertisers in a particular category the opportunity to have a "sponsored link" to their own site. Say you request "French vacation homes" as a search in Google; in addition to the standard list of sites, there will be paid-for links on the side of the page where you can click directly to the sponsor's own site (Fallowes, 2004).

REVIEW QUESTIONS

1. Compare and contrast the list you made for Question 2 in Chapter 7 with lists that people in the fourteen-to-eighteen-year-old range have. These people may be your younger siblings, the teacher's children, church youth groups, etc.
2. Make the same list and compare and contrast it with the list for a group of people eleven to thirteen.

Chapter 10

Ethnic Marketing and Marketing to the Disabled

ETHNIC MARKETING

Ethnic marketing works on the premise that people of the same ethnicity are more alike than they are like others of the same social class, psychographic profile, age, or whatever other segmenting variable one would prefer to use. I am not sure that this statement was ever true; in the early years of the twenty-first century, I am sure that it is not. That this is not a matter of academic interest, there are the following "truths" of the changing face of the United States (Schreiber, 2001, pp. ix-x):

1. By the year 2005, people of color will represent one-third of the American population; by 2050 they will be a majority.
2. Ethnic Americans (African, Hispanic, and Asian-Pacific) are increasing seven times as fast as the rest of the population.
3. Ethnic Americans have economic clout. Their spending power has doubled in the past decade and is now over $1 trillion.
4. Only about 1 to 2 percent of media spending is currently dedicated to targeted ethnic media.
5. Today's emerging ethnic consumers represent the largest, most overlooked market in America.
6. Many of today's ethnic Americans can be effectively reached at less cost than mainstream consumers. Many live in well-defined areas, consume well-defined media, and shop in certain retail outlets.

I do not doubt the truth of any of the previous statements. However, if we have learned anything over the years since World War II, it is the fact that the old ethnicities do soften if not completely erode over time because people move away from the old neighborhoods and marry people of different ethnicities, and the children have identities quite distinct from those of their parents. Tiger Woods's possible ethnic identification is quite complex, nor is he alone. The dilemma of identification of mixtures of mixtures will do nothing but increase as the twenty-first century unrolls. Ethnic media have always been important in the United States; foreign language newspapers published in the United States were long the backbone of ethnic identification. Most of them are gone now, as are the "old country" churches; in most cities there will still be services in the European languages, but people drive long distances to attend them, and not every church serving the old ethnicity can mount the foreign language service. The role played by the newspaper has been taken over by the radio, broadcasting news from the old country in both English and the old-country language. Because so many of these programs are now on public-broadcasting stations, however, the possibility of advertising to the old communities is reduced.

The new ethnicities of Hispanics and Carribbeans and Asians are more diffuse from the beginning. Hispanics are now in the United States in large numbers, but they come from Puerto Rico and Mexico and dozens of countries in Central and South America—not a unified population with a unified approach to much of anything. Cubans and Haitians are here in large numbers, but mostly confined geographically. Asians are hardly a unified group, as they comprise Chinese (both mainland and Taiwanese), Vietnamese, Thai, Indians, Bangladeshis, Pakastanis, Koreans, and Japanese—each with political and marketing identities separate from the artificial category of "Asian." Also, of course, what of the thousands of children from the Third World who were adopted by Americans during the 1980s and 1990s, ethnically Roumanian, Indian, Korean, but raised by "normal" American families; where will they fit in the future? Will they become more like their birth parents or their adoptive parents?

Diversity may be the hidden key to being a successful business in the new, changing America. General Motors has 28 percent of the market among black car buyers—leading the industry. It hosted the "GM All-Car Showdown" in February 2004, with black celebrities driving their Hummers and Cadillacs to compete for a promotional title (Hawkins, 2004). GM thought that perhaps it was going a bit too far, even though its Cadillac Escalade EXT—a very large luxury SUV—has become a hip-hop cultural icon. However, it has further placed a campaign in black print media consisting of a series of advertisements highlighting its black executives and its two black members of the board of directors. Other car manufacturers are trying to play catch-up in the face of this media campaign (Hawkins, 2004). Perhaps ethnic identification with a car model is something that a manufacturer needs to follow, but not try to lead.

Psychographics, of course, works from the premise that people in the psychographic segment are more alike than they are like others in different segments. If one believes in the validity of psychographics, as I do, then ethnic segmentation is less effective than psychographics—it is one of the demographic components. This is not to say that all of the models in an advertising campaign should be white and we can ignore the changing ethnicity in the United States—far from it. It is instead a plea to create color-blind messages, treat the segment as a universe, and then create the messages using whatever models best represent the segment. If a segment is 50 percent Mexican, it would behoove the marketer to ensure that Mexican models appeared in the advertisements. Fifty percent of the time? Not necessarily, but enough so that the Mexican population of that segment gets the message that they were included and deemed a valuable inclusion by the marketer.

MARKETING TO THE DISABLED

Disability is one of the demographic characteristics that also plays a part in people's psychographic makeup. There are a large number of physical disabilities, all of which change the way an individual deals with his or her environment; further complicating the issue is, of course, the distinction between being born with the disability or acquiring it later in life and having to make an adjustment to it and its consequences. Then there are the various mental disabilities, as well as the learning disabilities. All of these have marketing impacts. There are the obvious goods and services that apply only to those with certain disabilities; only people missing limbs are in the market for prosthetic limbs. We must again study the question, however, of who chooses versus who buys. However, there are goods and services that are not obvious because the disabilities are not; there is a large and growing market that has only recently emerged as the U.S. population is aging for items that make life easier for people who have arthritis in their hands—not crippling, but inconveniencing. If one lives alone and has difficulty opening jars because of arthritis, a jar opener may not be a life saver, but it certainly will increase the variety of foods available.

Often the goods and services bought for someone with a major disability are actually multiple buys across a family unit. I have a friend of many years' standing whose mother-in-law had had adult-onset polio in the 1950s, and by the time he married her daughter she was totally confined to a wheelchair. Her house was laid out and equipped for someone so confined; so was his, including a wheelchair ramp at the front door. Doing so made her visits easier for all concerned. To all appearances, someone living in the house was confined to a wheelchair, even though this was not true. Many of those with aging parents have lifting seats on the toilets in their houses for the ease of their parents when they come to visit. And so forth.

REVIEW QUESTIONS

1. List your ethnic ancestry as many generations back as you can. Compare the list with others in your class. Although it probably says much *about* you, do you think it is something a marketer can use?
2. Is ethnicity something a marketer should use for segmentation and marketing? Why or why not? What are the dangers inherent in this? The benefits?
3. What are the federally protected disabilities under the Americans with Disabilities Act? Why are these disabilities protected?
4. Are there benefits to the disabled in having their disabilities used as segmentation or marketing variables?

SECTION IV:
APPLICATIONS

This section explores how one firm, Douthit Communicaitons, Inc., has dealt with lifestyles over the past twenty years in creating its software to produce classified ads for used cars and houses. It has been a journey of discovery that is not over yet.

Any product with large amounts of emotional content—houses and cars of course, but also food and health care—can be amenable to lifestyle analysis and segmentation. Segmentation to simply divide a market is rarely profitable, and without profitability there is no point in segmentation.

doi:10.1300/5560_14

Chapter 11

Applying Autobiographical Memory to Advertising

Webber (1998, p. 9) puts his finger on two very important points, particularly for high-ticket items. First, for many products and services, customers may make an emotional decision and then go back and justify it intellectually—not only to others, but at least as much to themselves. Second, peer or social approval has real power on some customers' decisions to buy. How does this affect segmentation?

Sujan et al. (1993) address part of the problem of the affective nature of memory and how to transfer the affect to advertisement and brand judgments. They postulate on the basis of previous research that the retrieval of autobiographical memories changes consumers' thought processes so that there is more focus on personal memories and their associated affect and a reduced analysis of and memory for product attribute information. In two studies of student populations (this is not one of the times when I would object to using convenience samples of students) the authors tested eight hypotheses relating to evoking autobiographical memories. Their results go far beyond "nostalgia" ads and deal directly with "Remember the last time you . . .?" or the age-old "slice of life" commercials that played so well and so often in the early days of television. Anything that the marketer can do to evoke memory for use and activities in the consumer's mind rather than evoking the product itself will pay dividends as the consumer will see himself or herself using the product *again*. This is a return to creating habits. In their discussion of the limitations to their study and future research needs, the Sujan et al. (1993) state that the product chosen for their study (wine) "may have been particularly amenable to being linked to autobiographical episodes, and judgments of wine may be particularly influenced by available affect rather than product features"—particularly in such young wine drinkers with less sophistication and experience than their parents. But would cars not also fall into such a category? Or houses? Or food? Or most of the items that we buy and use? How affect driven is the purchase process? How attribute driven?

If Sujan et al. are correct that affect can obscure attributes, cueing the reader or viewer to autobiography first and then bringing in the features would create a more powerful advertisement for almost any product more expensive or complex than soap or chewing gum. Furthermore, Fournier and Guiry (1993) utilize preconsumption dreaming behavior in the formation of consumer "wish lists"; certainly this is an area that marketers can mine with profit. The role that advertisements can play in the dreaming is, of course, great, particularly for new-product advertising, and it has been tapped by many marketers in "product placements" in movies and television shows—venues that feed consumer dreams to begin with.

An article evocatively titled "Ask Not What the Brand Can Evoke; Ask What Can Evoke the Brand?" (Holden and Lutz, 1992) echoes the Sujan et al. article. Most research on memory and brand choice has assumed that the brand is available to be chosen. Holden and Lutz propose that it is necessary to examine the associations that led to retrieval of the brand instead of the brand that led to the associations. In addition, whereas brand evaluation focuses on what is evoked rather than on the cues, research on brand evocation needs to focus on the cues. What evokes a Ford Taurus in a consumer's mind? What evokes a Mercedes? A Colonial Revival house? Kentucky Fried Chicken? If we can find out the cues, we can present the consumer with an advertisement that evokes the product without having to be obvious or crude about it.

Ideally the customer should not be aware of why the advertisement so speaks "Taurus;" however, the ad should not even suggest a car so similar to the Taurus as its identical twin, the Mercury Sable. This is not manipulation of the consumer but rather making the advertising an integrated whole that fits together and is aimed at one segment (or a few) and is designed to send other segments away, in both cases with consumers not really knowing why. This is the wholeness of psychographic segmentation, the promise of using what we know to lead consumers in a direction that they want to go in the first place— in other words, using segmentation to live up to the promise of the Marketing Concept's selling people what they want to buy.

Chapter 12

The Tribes:
A New Psychographic Scheme

After a period of using commercially available segmentation schemes, Douthit Communications, Inc. (DCI), had become dissatisfied with changes in the scheme and with the support it was getting from research provided by the vendor. The decision was made in late 1990 to develop a proprietary scheme for residential real estate similar to the syndicated scheme it was currently using. American LIVES was retained and conducted a random-sample mail survey of the Denver, Colorado, real estate market (American LIVES, 1991); Denver was then and still is one of the bigger markets for DCI's *Homes Illustrated* division of homes-for-sale magazines, as well as the headquarters of ReMax, Inc., a major national real estate brokerage firm. The survey sampled Denver housing sales for the previous eighteen months. Of 1,153 valid names and addresses of recent house buyers acquired from a mailing list service to whom surveys were mailed, there was a return of approximately 500 questionnaires, for a 43 percent response rate. American LIVES deemed the response rate adequate for all the statistical analyses to be performed for its segmentation study.

The survey asked questions never before systematically examined in a real estate context, although some had previously been asked in research performed for DCI. The questionnaire was jointly developed by DCI personnel and American LIVES, although it was not tested before it was fielded. The instrument was eleven pages long (much too long according to all the rules of thumb in the marketing research field—the return rate is astronomical in the face of this fact), and it explored many unclear items that American LIVES hoped would lead to shorter questionnaires in future studies. The American LIVES survey is unique in that it covers the house-search process, desire for house features, and use of the house by different segments, house style analyses, and values and demographics (the LIVES analysis proper—Lifestyle, Interests, Values, Expectations, and Symbols of the house buyer).

The questionnaire was designed with several kinds of questions that, when taken together, give a rich basis for the analysis and segmentation:

- Why they moved
- The house search process
- Type, size, and price of house
- How they sold their previous house
- Intentions for the next time they sell a house
- Preference for new or previously owned house
- Attitudes toward realtors and their quality of service
- Information and services used in the house search
- Preferences for neighborhood and area features
- Preferences for exterior and interior features
- Different uses for rooms
- Values, lifestyles, and demographics

The LIVES segmentation model follows two principles (American LIVES, 1991). First, all people organize their lives around their values and lifestyles. Different groups in the population employ very different values and lifestyles; the use of the values and lifestyle measures gives very stable market segments that are based on what anthropologists and sociologists call *subcultures.* Second, consumers try to make their lives more meaningful and consistent in terms of a few basic ideas. The segmentation scheme does not have to come up with a large list of descriptors of peoples' ways of life, for some ideas are more basic than others. If this sounds somewhat like the VALS segmentation principles discussed earlier, perhaps it is because one of the developers of the LIVES scheme worked for VALS while Arnold Mitchell was still alive. Perhaps that also helps to explain why the LIVES scheme seems to make sense.

American LIVES then produced the segmentation that was tied specifically to Denver and yet could also satisfy DCI's strategic needs for the *Homes Illustrated* magazine markets as well as its software for writing real estate classified advertisements, which is sold under various names at different times. The primary applications of a LIVES segmentation are in a wide variety of business whose products are complex or expensive, symbolically loaded, a key part of someone's lifestyle, reflective of what is most meaningful in consumers' lives and sold differently to different groups. Examples of products or service that this approach would work well for include cars, consumer electronics, and vacation travel. Houses also obviously fit the bill. The returned questionnaires were analyzed along the underlying dimensions of what is most important in the lives of the house buyers; five subcultures, which where christened "Tribes" for ease of communication, were discovered: Winners, Authenticks, Wannabes (now called "Trenders"), Heartlanders, and Maintainers (called "Upkeepers" for a number of years but rechristened in 2004 "Self-Sufficient"[1]).

Winners represented 23 percent of the market and were the most upscale group in the survey. Seventy-six percent of the Winners were managers and professionals, 68 percent had incomes in 1990 over $50,000 (versus 38 percent of those surveyed) and 21 percent had incomes over $100,000, and 50 percent had attended or completed graduate school. The median age was thirty-eight years, the same as those surveyed, and 60 percent were male. This group was highly status and success oriented; they were business conservatives. This group dominated the high-priced house market for both new houses and resales. They liked all the status features in a house and liked to have a luxury look in as many rooms as possible. They wanted a "Big House," a trophy house in a mature, status neighborhood.

Winners are the most visible buyers in the real estate market. Realtors and home builders are extremely familiar with this segment because they most identify with Winners. Winners focus their attention on self, work, and family, in that order. They are knowledgeable and savvy house buyers who know what they want and want to buy it efficiently. They are materialistic to a fault and technologically aware. Their house needs to reflect their sense of themselves: stylish and good-looking. They want to see a large variety of styles and front elevations and want a lot of choices in what they buy—houses and otherwise. In some cases, neither the neighborhood nor the outlook matters to Winners; all that matters is the house itself. Even houses with views of rail yards and landfills, if they are priced high enough and are big enough, will sell to Winners (Hagerty and Kim, 2004).

Authenticks represented 18 percent of the market; they were the second most upscale group. Fifty-three percent were managers and professionals, and 45 percent had 1990 incomes over $50,000; 27 percent attended or completed graduate school. Half of Authenticks are men. This group is dominant in the "preowned-house-in-an-established-neighborhood" market. Their house is expected to be a nest, hidden away from the world, with no big statement to the street or any status or luxury features inside or out.

Authenticks are individualists, for all their broad social concerns, so their tastes are more personal than those of other groups. They care more about being unique than they do in owning what is unique. They are well educated, creative, and self-confident. They are psychologically sophisticated, with a low tolerance for being "sold to"; many hate builders and realtors and feel that these people are dumb and have poor taste and the wrong values to deal with Authenticks. Their house is a way for them to show their creativity, so they want a house that they can invest with their own personal touch and their own meanings and values.[2] Family is less important to Authenticks, and this often shows in their house choices—their values in general are nontraditional.

Heartlanders represented 21 percent of the market. This is the oldest Tribe, with a median age of forty-one years; almost one third of Heartlanders were over fifty. Partly because of their age, they dominated the empty-nester market. Their income was average ($35,000), their education level slightly lower—high school with some college. Heartlanders were 35 percent male. The median price of their house was right on the median of the sample, but they had more equity built up in the house, partly because of their age but also partly because they were less apt to refinance to withdraw cash from the house for other purposes and less apt to move. They wanted to be in built-up, very-accessible parts of the city, but the neighborhoods must be safe and secure, because this Tribe is very concerned about crime on the street. A "plain-vanilla" house would do—simple, comfortable, and practical, with no status features. Their notion of a house is extremely conventional and conformist: they will reject all of the innovative features that attract the Authenticks, partly because they are new but also partly because they hold the Authenticks and their values in contempt.

Heartlanders are conformists who lack broad social concerns, with very little personalization of taste. They are traditionalists who do not feel comfortable in the modern world, who want their path through life to be narrow, well lit, and well posted by authority figures whom they respect. They long for a nostalgic, idealized image of the way things were in small towns around 1900; when Csikszentmihalyi and Rochberg-Halton and their interviewers visited the houses of people who were probably in this Tribe, the objects they found in the living rooms were old, family oriented (pictures and memorabilia), and freighted with provenance—the objects were in transition from generation to generation and did not truly seem to belong to their current owners (Csikszentmihalyi and Rochberg-Halton, 1981). The religious right is strongest in this Tribe; they are intolerant of both the Winners' emphasis on what Heartlanders see as greed, materialism, and status display and the Authenticks' "way-outness." They seek to surround themselves with clear, well-marked boundaries that show that they live in an unchanged, safe haven.

Trenders, representing 23 percent of the market, were the youngest Tribe, with a median age of thirty-six years; about one quarter were under thirty years. The median income was $31,000, and they had below-average education, in part reflective of their youth. Their occupations were mostly sales, services, and technical support; 41 percent were male. The median house price was $72,000, the lowest of any Tribe; most have had to settle grudgingly for less of a house than they wanted. They wanted to have locations close to work and shopping. They expected to overextend themselves financially to buy their house, and they did. They lusted for nearly all house features, especially status and luxury, but had to settle for "plain vanilla" because it was all they could afford. They wanted a nest hidden from the world, but with a front elevation that would make a big statement to the world, even if that big front was just a façade. Given that the house would be smaller than they wanted and below-average in price, Trenders were caught in the cleft stick of conflicting wants.

Trenders are imitators of Winners and define their lifestyles, values, and house preferences in terms of what they perceive Winners to have, want, and be. Actually, they do not have a clear vision of what the Winners are, have, do, or want. Instead, they operate from a stereotypical set of attitudes formed at a distance, so the features they want are exaggerated. Their vision of the "good life" is what Winners have—period. They are obsessed with status and success, but do not understand the cues. They are young and ambitious, but their lack of education will tend to work against them for the rest of their lives. Ongoing income constraints will prevent them from getting much of what they want in material terms; thus they define the bottom of the previously owned house market. Their champagne tastes, which are longings rather than experiences, confront the dismal fact of their current and future beer budgets. They simply lack the education and job skills to move up.

Self-Sufficients represented 16 percent of the sample; this was the most downscale group, with many blue-collar workers. Their median income was, like the Trenders, $31,000, but Self-Sufficients had even lower education: high school, yes, and even some college (but less college than the Trenders and, given a median age of thirty-nine years, their college education was probably completed unless through job transition they went back to college for a career change). The median price of their house was $76,000, well below the sample, but 5 percent higher than that of the Trenders. They wanted fewer features than other Tribes and wanted them less strongly. What they appear to want is the small, cheap, plain, "fixer-upper" house—basic shelter. They were the Tribe most likely to buy a "For Sale by Owner" house to save on the real estate agent's commission. They, like the Trenders, wanted locations that were close to shopping and work. In many respects, Self-Sufficients are simply Trenders who have aged and know that they have lost the possibility of succeeding, although with a 53 percent male population, the gender split is significantly different from that of the Trenders.

The Self-Sufficients are often the people who fix your car or paint your house. Life has passed them by and they know it; they are cynical, alienated, and discouraged about values. The few positive responses Self-Sufficients made to value statements were patriotism, macho attitudes, and sports. Male Self-Sufficients are less interested in family life. Physical activities such as sports, hunting, fishing, and tinkering with cars or the house, as well as watching television, are likely to define their leisure time. It appears that they see the values espoused by other groups as a sham, and they are unalterably opposed to the values espoused by Authenticks. They define the bottom of the preowned house market. They are also the least likely to see real estate agents or read a homes magazine—or, in fact, to read much of anything. Print is not the medium to use to communicate with Self-Sufficients; it remains to be seen if the Internet might be, but in the meantime it seems that the medium of choice would be front-yard signage for them to see as they drive by.

The Tribes segmentation scheme was immediately taken to heart by DCI. Within a couple of months of its completion, a presentation on the Tribes was ready to show to the real estate firms that were DCI's biggest customers at the time, and the people who saw the presentation generally sat and nodded their agreement about the Tribes' hitting the nail on the head; these were their customers. This was basically the identical reaction to that of the same group of people when they were exposed to VALS, further increasing my feeling that the Tribes scheme works

The survey and its results are truly confined to Denver, Colorado, in the early 1990s; the survey has never been replicated, nor was its geographic extent enlarged at the time—despite pleas from me and others that both things be done. Nevertheless, with this caveat in mind, I believe that the basic Tribes structure still is valid. The median incomes and house prices for each Tribe, of course, need to be adjusted for thirteen years of inflation and for different geographic areas. The exact percentage mix of each Tribe in each market will differ (which is true of any scheme with a national reach when it is brought down to a locality), and, were one to use the Tribes as a "segmentation for design" or "segmentation for sales" scheme, it would be important to find the percentages in each market; VALS contractors made these numbers available for local markets (WJW-TV8, 1988). DCI has not used the Tribes for either of these purposes, so its surface validity is more important to the firm than its statistical validity. The surface validity of the Tribes continues to be verified as group after group in various parts of the country is exposed to the Tribes and, almost universally, the heads in the room nod.

REVIEW QUESTIONS

1. Reread the definitions of the Tribes. Which Tribe are you in? Why do you think that?

2. Log onto the Internet. Go to www.AdWriter.com and take the Tribes quiz. What Tribe does the computer say you are in?
3. Are the results for Questions 1 and 2 the same? If not, why not?
4. Are you more comfortable with deciding which Tribe you are in yourself or being told by the computer? Why?

Chapter 13

Single-Family Houses

One of the truisms of segmentation strategy is that using the scheme has to be more profitable than marketing without it, net of the expense of developing and using the scheme itself. In many cases, this means that segmentation for low-priced items, unless sold in very large quantities, is not truly feasible, even though it might be interesting. Given the price of houses, and the fact that the commission to the firms selling those houses typically runs into several thousands of dollars, segmenting should be profitable if the scheme works. Using lifestyle and psychographic segmentation schemes, even though they cost more than other kinds, is advisable because of the enormous psychological baggage that houses carry for so many Americans.

Not only are our houses typically the most expensive item we will ever buy (cars come a distant second), but we have major psychological involvement with them. Clare Cooper Marcus has spent most of her working life dealing with people who have psychological difficulties with their houses, often because of conflicts between the house they are currently living in and the one they want to be living in or the location where they would prefer to live. Also, they carry deep and abiding memories (happy and otherwise) of previous houses, and these trigger memories of the relationships they had with the people they shared them with (Cooper, 1976, 1978; Marcus, 1995). We personalize the space. Agreeing with Csikszentmihalyi and Rochberg-Halton (1981), Marcus (1995, p. 11) wrote that "[more] and more I found . . . that it is the moveable objects in the home, rather than the physical fabric itself, that are the symbols of self." Fiffer and Fiffer (1995) support Marcus's contention by examining what nineteen American authors remember about rooms in the houses where they spent their childhoods; universally, it was the contents of the built environment that marked turning points. However, it is not always the contents that enable the memories; sometimes it is the house.

> Our [American] literature reiterates with remarkable consistency the centrality of the house in American cultural life and imagination. In many of our major novels, a house stands at stage center as a unifying symbolic structure that represents and defines the relationships of the central characters to one another, to themselves, and to the world and raises a wide range of questions starting with Thoreau's deceptively simple "What is a house?" . . . Behind the myth [of the self-sufficient man building his own house] lies the enduring idea that a man's house represents his self . . . and becomes, as it grows into a home, a direct extension of that self into the enduring media of wood and stone. (Chandler, 1991, pp. 1, 2)

Even at the end of life this centrality of the house remains. My mother recently had to move from the house she shared with my father for the past twenty years into an adult foster-care home. We had moved repeatedly while I was growing up; the house in Eugene, Oregon, was the eighth house they had owned or rented since my father returned from World War II. It carried extra emotional baggage for my mother because my father died in their bedroom, but my mother had said repeatedly for years that she wanted to be able to die there. Unfortunately, such was an impossibility as she got older and more frail. When she moved to the foster home, however, she was able to take her bed, a dresser, her television, chairs, and some paintings and was able to recreate a simulacrum of her house in her new room. In so doing, she was able to leave the house willingly, if not happily. We tend to acquire and display possessions for the purpose of feeling differentiated, of being different from others; we use them to attempt to enhance our self-perception of uniqueness, which allows marketers much scope (Tian et al., 2001).[1]

How do all of these psychology of houses affect their segmentation? One way to think about it is the difference between the fabric of the "house"—the building itself—and the contents of the "home"—the interior and its contents thought of in psychological terms. When the focus groups discussed in the Case in Chapter 19 were talking, the different groups used the words "house" and "home" in not-exactly-synonymous ways. The Achievers were clearly "house" oriented—size of the house, its impressiveness and that of the neighborhood, its potential for price appreciation and resale value—in short, the house's "curb appeal" was uppermost in their discussion. For Belongers, the "house" mattered little except for a physical shell around the family's "home." They mentioned family space—kitchen and yard—as well as proximity to church, school, and relatives. The Inner Directeds seemed to care little about the house—or even, in some respects, the home. They wanted an established interesting neighborhood with a diverse cross section of people. Then, and only then, did they show much interest in the details and rooms of the house.

The difference between "house" and "home" should mean something, but it is "by and large the linguistic waste product of the American real-estate industry" (Hollander, 1993, p. 37). The split is also a concept that may have meaning only in a Germanic language. The relationship between "house"—the building—and "home"—the more general condition of where you live and have your focus—is *not* identical. If Robert Frost is right that "home is where, when you go there they have to take you in," it does not necessarily take a building for the statement to be true; what Frost is really talking about is a family. Although we in the United States may have lost the linguistic distinction between house and home, many of the participants in the focus groups, many of the people that Jack Nasar's (1988a) researchers showed the pictures to, many of Clare Cooper Marcus's interviewees were struggling to resurrect the distinction and to give it meaning again.

When the American LIVES survey was fielded in the early 1990s, there was no World Wide Web. Real estate information consisted of real estate classified ads in the newspapers, illustrated homes guides, slick magazines for upper-end houses, television shows with the occasional tour of the inside of the house (again, for the upper-end houses), and real estate agents. Time and again, the American LIVES respondents, particularly those in higher income brackets, complained bitterly about the information available about houses, feeling it to be far inferior to product information that was available to them for other items that they bought. They particularly resented the role that real estate agents played in the information stream, feeling that the agent deliberately withheld and distorted information at every step of the process.[2] In 2003, with the World Wide Web's having become strong and a major player in the information and search processes, Douthit Communications fielded two focus groups (one of males and one of females) to see what the status of information in residential real estate had become: The firm was in the process of developing and evaluating a search portal for use by consumers in the real estate market and felt that it had become necessary to identify the needs and to understand the expectations of individuals in the market since the Internet had become such an important medium.

Each group began with a discussion about what sources of information participants had used in the home-buying search process as well as the order of each method used. Most participants said they used online services, the newspaper, real estate magazines, open house events, a real estate agent, and driving through a neighborhood. However, the classified section of the Sunday newspaper was the starting point of choice.

Littlefield et al. (2000) list six sources from a survey that was fielded in the late 1990s: brokers/agents was first, followed by newspapers, friends and relatives, the Internet, flyers and other postings, and other sources, such as cable television and driving around. Specific Web sites were brought up during the focus groups and discussed, ranging from Realtor.com (the site of the National Association of Realtors) to specific sites run by specific agents. The members mentioned search patterns on various sites that turned out upon investigation not to be possible; also, the members felt that Web sites were not being updated as frequently as other media, that houses that were sold remain on the Web to "entice" people to contact the agent. Although everyone in both groups had used the Internet for searching for a house to some extent, and all the members had recently bought a house or were looking to buy a house, not a single member of either group had bought a house he or she had seen on the Internet (National Market Measures, 2003).

If one expands the information that buyers are looking for from specific houses and prices to school district information, what else is in the neighborhood, shopping centers, available walking tours of the neighborhood or the house, taxes, and so forth, the Internet becomes a much more important information source. It has been found that significant relationships exist among consumers' awareness, access, age, and their use of the Internet in their recent home purchase; this fact suggests that real estate firms should advertise their sites to buyers and what kinds of information are available there. Most people who have used the Internet to search for their current house "perceive the Internet to be very effective in aiding their home purchase. This perceived effectiveness would stimulate them to use the Internet in future home purchases" (Littlefield et al., 2000, p. 586). Although this research does not quite square with the focus groups (some of the differences can be explained by differences in location and time—the Littlefield et al. research was fielded in Virginia in the 1990s, and DCI's focus groups were in Cleveland, Ohio, in 2003—type of research—focus group versus survey—and so on, the results are similar enough to show that the Internet will continue to be a source of real estate information.

How to make the Internet work for real estate? Even though most house listings are now on the Internet (frequently on many different sites: Realtor.com, the firm's site, the listing agent's site, etc.), the listing data are driven by the needs of the specific Multiple Listing Service to mention size of the house and lot, number of bedrooms and baths, etc. There is little or no concern for what other information the buyers would like to see before they make the decision to come look at the house. Many house listings now also offer a virtual tour of the inside of the house so that the potential buyer can "walk" through the house prior to deciding to see it. Obviously, if one wants buyers to look at a product, one has to advertise features and benefits that buyers want; real estate, however, is driven by the sellers, for whom the entire industry is organized and around whom everything revolves. This makes for strange information and advertising decisions.

The American LIVES (1991) survey, mentioned earlier, also sought to discover what the different Tribes wanted in a house—less about architectural style than about how people and families use the structure to live in. The analysis was conducted along seven dimensions: wanting a luxury look to the house; wanting particular interior status features; wanting a house to be "open, light, and airy"; wanting a house that is a nest; wanting to make heavy use of the living room for everyday living; wanting a large, well-equipped kitchen; and wanting a large or fancy master bath. The clumping of specific features into meaningful clusters of features was performed by people with several decades of total experience in the real estate business.

The clustering analysis produced seven different house types (see Table 13.1 for descriptions and distribution statistics as of 1991). The

TABLE 13.1. House type descriptions, 1991.

House type	Description	Percentage
1	Want the basic, plain-vanilla house; do not care about open, light, and airy	31
2	Want open, light, and airy; emphasize the living room; do not care about a big, well-equipped kitchen	18
3	Really want luxury look; emphasize the living room	11
4	Really want interior status features; emphasize the living room	8
5	Really want a fancy master bath; really want a nest; want big, well-equipped kitchen; do not care about luxury look, interior status features, or open, light, and airy	8
6	Really want open, light, and airy; want big, well-equipped kitchen; emphasize family room; do not care about luxury look	9
7	Really want big, well-equipped kitchen; emphasize living room; do not care for a nest	12

Source: American LIVES, 1991.

Note: The percentages are not of housing stock but rather percentages of the respondents who want this house type. Total does not equal 100 percent because of rounding error.

analysis attempted to match the House Types to the Tribes but without a great deal of confidence in the results.[3] Too many of the Tribes have significantly high scores for wanting more than one of the house types. Although I had seen the same results of Types wanting more than one kind of house in a set of focus groups done for a client trying to match VALS types with architectural styles (see Case, Chapter 19), the house types, because they were psychographically derived based on features in the house, should have been more differentiated. The house types and their percentages presented in Table 13.1 refer to the people who talked about them, not existing housing stock; this, of course, is a problem if one wants to map house types to the Tribes, because it is possible that the house types will not be found in houses that real estate agents will have listed. Although a computer program could be created to take the house features as listed by the agents and work them into the clusters that are the house types, there has to be a cleaner, easier way to deal with this issue.

We spent much time and quite a bit of corporate resources to work on this issue, with some success. Table 13.2 shows the descriptions as of 2004. The differences between the original descriptions and the current ones are striking. They have been fleshed out, detached from new construction or any geographic region. More important, the features that drive a house into one type and not into another have been codified and scored, and a list of houses can now be sorted by house type. This feat is demonstrated on the Internet every day at several sites that can be viewed by the public (cbcol.theexternet.com/hometypes; cbfl.theexternet.com/hometypes being only two that are available as I write this).

There are indications that people who are looking for houses will use the house-type sorting. In focus groups held in 2003 and described in the Case in Chapter 19, the members of the group were told about the house-type sorts and indicated that they would be interested in using it (National Market Measures, 2003). This fact, of course, ties into the Littlefield et al. (2000) model of Internet information usage; the ability to sort houses—beyond location, price, and features—is an attractive concept to house buyers. There are several people per day who navigate to the House Type sections of the two Web sites mentioned earlier; there is little attention drawn to them on the screen, for corporate reasons, but people do manage to get there and seem to be using the tool presented.

After twenty years of consulting in the real estate business, mostly with buyers but some work also with agents, it is clear to me that the information currently provided to house buyers is not only insufficient in quantity and quality for their wants but also not up to the quality and quantity that is available for other purchases. The American LIVES survey in 1991 specifically found this to be true, as has every research instrument or focus group with which I have been involved. Littlefield et al. (2000) hope that the Internet and the vast amount of information available there will remedy the situation. However, without some methods to filter through the high noise-to-information ratio, the Internet will prove not to be the benefit that it could have been. Sorting by Tribes (or some other segmentation scheme) would help filter out houses that appeal to other segments but not to one's own

TABLE 13.2. House types, 2004.

Label	Description
Luxury Look	A large "show-off" home, the external appearance and verdant setting of which will convey a sense of wealth and status. The interior is luxuriously appointed, providing everything from attractive bedroom suites to special-activity areas, including ample space for entertaining. Luxury look homes are often "monumental" in style, embracing Tudor, Georgian, or Greek Revival design—and may be set in professionally landscaped, parklike grounds. There are, of course, Luxury Look condominiums as well, which feature similarly luxurious space and amenities, including beautiful grounds.
Big Outlook	A bright, airy, Contemporary-style home that features an open-concept floorplan with a major focus on windowed views. Whether the home is large or small, two-story or single-level. It is certain to boast glass walls—or very large windows—that "bring the outdoors in" and a look out from its major rooms to interesting garden or woodland views, or to spectacular panoramas of water/mountains or city lights. Similarly, high-rise condominiums with vivid views are choice homes for those enthralled by Big Outlooks.
Traditional Lovers	Whether a cottage or a mansion, if it is an updated or new version of Victorian, Colonial, or Spanish design, it suggests another, gentler age. The formality of a center hall and the separate dining and living rooms are offset by the comforts of family—or keeping—rooms that provide a sense of warmth and security. Traditional homes will usually offer the warmth of at least one fireplace, perhaps several, and many will allow the summer delights of old-fashioned porches or wrap-around verandahs, and the winter comfort of a sunroom or solarium.
Gathering Place	Its exterior may be posh or plain, but, whatever its style, this home's bywords are comfort and hospitality. The interior is sure to be light and airy, casual and open, welcoming kids, kith and kin, and friends. A big, open, dine-in kitchen, large living room, perhaps a formal dining room, and a family room with fireplace help to cater to crowds and family. The Gathering Place home is also likely to have an outdoor grill, a generous patio, and perhaps a swimming pool or poolhouse or cabana, and possibly a tennis court available to guests and family.
Cozy Nest	The ideal home for "shut-out-the-world" folks, the Cozy Nest may be a smaller home or cottage in a quiet neighborhood, or a larger townhome or condominium, or yet a rustic retreat on an acreage—but its chief virtue is that it offers a warm, enclosed feeling, a sense of privacy and provides a true refuge from the world. The Cozy Nest interior may be simple or full of luxury amenities, computer equipment and art objects—whatever its owner wishes to make of it.

TABLE 13.2 *(continued)*

Label	Description
Sensibly Simple	A smaller home without special frills, but containing all the basic conveniences at an affordable price. The Sensibly Simple home may well be a fix-up home or a nicely kept home in a settled neighborhood, or perhaps a home sited on a small acreage. The ideal "start-up" home, it offers newlyweds and other individuals who want home ownership advantages the opportunity to "own your own" without excessive costs.
Hidden Treasures	Typically, a recently built, two-story home, its exterior reveals little to the street save for a gable roofline, a three-car garage, and perhaps a high Palladian window above its foyer. All attention boyond a small landscaped front yard is devoted to the home's interior and its back garden, featuring decks or patios. The interior provides the latest in gourmet kitchens, up-to-the-minute baths and spacious master suites. And, of course, ideal Hidden Treasure homes are also in condominiums and townhomes which present nothing of themselves to the street, but may contain delightful amenities and objets d'art set in well-designed space.

Source: The Externet (cbcol.theexternet.com).

segment and keep them out of sight. Sorting by house type could do likewise.

REVIEW QUESTIONS

1. Describe in detail the house you live(d) in with your parents: number of stories, rooms, bathrooms, bedrooms. Be as detailed as possible. Compare your list with those of the rest of the class.
2. Describe your ideal house in the same detail that you did in Question 1.
3. In class, list the descriptions of the houses in Question 2. Are there clumps of similar houses described by students? Are those groupings of houses the same as the groupings by Tribe? How are they similar or different?

Chapter 14

Used Cars

Almost from the beginning of the development of ReAd and its predecessors, DCI paralleled the development of a similar program to write advertisements for automobiles. The development process was similar, and by 1989 development had reached the stage where significant money and effort would be needed if DCI were to proceed with development and marketing of the program that was tentatively called AutoAd.

The decision was made in October 1989 to convene a focus group of used-car managers from car dealerships in Cleveland, Ohio, and let them see the program, use it, and write advertisements. There were major technical difficulties with this group. First, all of the managers were from firms that advertised in one or the other of two newspapers controlled by DCI, so it was hardly a random sample even within the usual constraints of focus groups. Second, the moderator was badly trained on the program because DCI was unable to deliver a working version of the program until noon of the day of the focus group; when the time came to show off the program, she had great difficulty in so doing. Third, the focus group guide was never prepared to final draft, so it was almost an unfocused focus group.

None of these problems truly mattered. Within the first ten minutes of the group, it was obvious that AutoAd was not going to be a product that this market could or would use. First, the managers resented the amount of information that would have to be entered into the form to produce the advertisement; we had heard the same complaint from real estate agents who had to type in a whole form for the Multiple Listing Service and then repeat the process for ReAd. Second, the fact that AutoAd could produce many unique ads for different media was immaterial for them; they wrote one ad and placed it in the local daily newspaper, the weekly newspaper, the *Trader,* and elsewhere—

despite the fact that different advertisements in different media might produce better results in each medium. Third, and probably most important, the managers stated unanimously that AutoAd did not fit in with the way they worked—"recognition of a technological opportunity in the absence of a clear organizational need to be served by such innovation is not likely to lead to successful implementation" (Bikson et al., 1981, p. 28). In other words, if the customers do not see a need for a product, they are unlikely to buy it. Solving this problem was what I have called "missionary marketing" (Cahill, 1995a).

The managers also felt they did not need the program. Universally they said that they wrote their ads by getting in a car when they bought it for the lot and driving it around the block; by the time they got back to the used-car lot, they knew what to say. Most used-car ads at this time were feature driven: make, model, mileage, color, condition. The fact that AutoAd might write a "better" ad did not sway them. The fact that AutoAd could write advertisements in multiple formats for multiple media did not sway them. The fact that AutoAd could write different ads for substantially similar cars did not sway them. As one of the managers said, if he were the manager at a particular dealership with "fifty identical Chevy Cavaliers," he might be interested, but because he only had "unique" cars he would have no interest in AutoAd. In short, the focus group served mostly to allow DCI to stop the development of AutoAd before more corporate resources were spent on a product that clearly was not going to meet a need for the market to which it was to be targeted; development of AutoAd was terminated before the end of 1989 and the program was mothballed.

Development was reopened in 1997. By this time, the original AutoAd software was so old it had ossified; it was written in Better Basic to run on an IBM PC/XT under MS-DOS, and the computing environment by 1997 was completely different. The first step to opening AutoAd's further development would seem to be a programming upgrade, but I managed to stop that and get an allocation of funds to do some research, given the reason that development was stopped in 1989. Reprogramming into a Windows environment would make no sense if the product was still unmarketable. Much more important was research into marketability.

While marketability research was in process, DCI was able to join in a national survey fielded by Bruskin-Goldring Research (1997) with a large automobile manufacturer and a large car rental firm on the subject of the automobile-buying decision process between new cars and used. The underlying sponsors of the study were interested in the new versus used, because resales had reached almost 50 percent of all purchases and leases, partly as the result of many decisions made by the manufacturers to push lease programs and make sales to their rental subsidiaries, who were then forced to sell "new-used" cars every six months as new cars were shipped to them by the manufacturers. Because DCI was a subscriber, we were enabled to add specific questions to the questionnaire.

The used-vehicle buyer had been frequently studied before (Newspaper Association of America, 1995). Two years before the Bruskin-Goldring study, the "average" used-vehicle buyer was younger than the overall population, 60 percent of the buyers of used vehicles were male, 60 percent were married, 50 percent were from households with two adults, 78 percent of the buyers already owned at least one car, and 50 percent of the buyers acknowledged that someone else shared in the purchasing decision.

What the Bruskin-Goldring study did that was new was to go into the total automobile market and look at the buyers as a whole, whether they bought new cars or used. Using attitudinal measures, the study came up with three segments: Loyal Used Buyers, Loyal New Buyers, and Fence Sitters. The surprise finding was that each segment represented approximately one-third of the market. (Table 14.1 gives the demographics of the segments; Exhibit 14.1 gives the behavioral dimensions.) It is, however, the Fence Sitters who are most important for any growth in used-car sales, as well as for the burgeoning onrush of advertising media aimed at used-car buyers on Web sites, in used-car magazines, and in newspaper classified sections. Fence Sitters are ambivalent toward whether to buy a used or a new car, although the survey found that they were more likely to buy a new car (62 versus 38 percent); but *buy* cars they do—overwhelmingly, they are more apt to buy than lease. The deciding factor for this segment was relative price, what the deal was on "equivalence," although another reason that appeared quite strongly (particularly for Fence Sitters) was certification or warranty. When the survey was fielded, there were large numbers of cars hitting the used-car market coming off of lease and other programs (particularly from the rental companies owned by car manufacturers) with several years remain-

TABLE 14.1. Demographics of the automobile-buying segments.

	Used-car buyers	Loyal used	New-car buyers	Loyal new	Fence sitters	U.S. population
Sex (%)						
Male	44	46	45	43	45	48
Female	56	54	55	57	55	52
Age (%)						
18-34	27	27	23	25	21	33
35-49	41	37	40	39	44	30
50+	32	36	37	36	29	34
Mean	45	45.9	47.1	46.6	46	44.4
Income (%)						
<$30K	18	17	9	12	19	47
$30K<50K	30	25	21	22	25	26
$50K<100K	40	47	55	46	48	21
>$100K	12	11	14	20	8	6
Mean (000)	60.1	61.6	69.3	71.1	63.3	40.9
Education (%)						
High school	32	26	33	35	36	52
Some college	26	27	22	19	24	25
College plus	35	40	42	42	34	21

Source: Bruskin-Goldring Research (1997).

EXHIBIT 14.1. Attitudinal Measures

I take pride in my car's appearance.
A well-maintained used car is as good as a new car.
I would rather own a used car than lease a new car.
Used cars are a better value than new cars.
Your car is a reflection of your personality.
Buying a car is one of life's more painful purchases.
It would be great if I could buy a car without a salesperson helping.
Buying a used car means buying someone else's problems.

Source: Bruskin-Goldring Research, 1997

ing on the original manufacturer's warranty, giving those who bought these cars an additional level of security in the reliability of the used car.

So here is a segmentation scheme, based on good, solid research that was both demographic and behavioral. Because the segments are all the same size and there are only three of them, they are large enough to be profitable; ongoing research could be relatively inexpensive, although the original research project was not. The three segments are different demographically and behaviorally, and one of them can be ignored by firms that deal only with new cars, and one can be ignored by firms that deal only with used cars. It is the middle segment, the Fence Sitters, who might be difficult. Because they seem to represent the only segment from which significant used-car sales growth would come from, it behooves any marketer to address them and their needs.

This should not be difficult. The sticking point for the Fence Sitters to buying a used car is not so much price as a concern over lifecycle cost. Used cars need more repairs sooner after purchase, on average, than new cars, and new cars come with warranties from the manufacturers—longer now than ever before. Given the large number of used cars that are "program cars"—coming off leases rather than from an "owner"—the new car now tends to be much younger than in the 1970s and 1980s. The younger age coupled with the longer manufacturers' warranty means that many used cars now have manufacturers' warranty left on them—sometimes as much as four or five years. This fact would make a Fence Sitter more likely to buy such a car; reliability issues bear a lower financial risk to the purchaser. A wise dealer could take a car with, say, four years of its manufacturer's warranty left, add three years of nontransferable dealer warranty to it, and sell the car with a seven-year warranty. The warranty costs to the dealer five to seven years out would be reduced by the fact that if the buyer sells the car, the warranty expires. More research could be done to determine what other serious issues Fence Sitters have with used cars in general. How to reach them? No segmentation scheme is complete without a way to communicate with the segments. Although advertisements in the classified section of the newspapers emphasizing the warranty program might help, it would probably be better to take out special display ads in nontraditional sections of the paper explaining that there are many "late model, low mileage used cars with lots of warranty" available at the dealer. This should appeal to the Fence Sitters.

Is this the best segmentation scheme possible? At the time of the survey, advertising and marketing of used cars was almost a research black hole, in line with the unresearched nature of most items primarily sold through classified advertising. The various newspaper trade groups had some inkling of who their target audience was, but there was no connection made between the reader of classified advertising and the buyer of the used car, whether the car was for sale by a dealer or by the owner. The Bruskin-Goldring survey made some connection, as there were questions related specifically to the media used by the respondents to shop. The automobile manufacturers spend billions of dollars on advertising the cars when they are new (with questionable effectiveness—see Buzzell and Baker, 1972), but then these cars "disappear" into advertising that talks about make, model, color, and mileage as they are driven from the showroom. Worse, car ads have become reduced to "technobabble," mimicking the personal-computer ads with their focus on features that readers do not understand (Witcher, 1988).

What is even worse, the manufacturers were missing what was becoming a large proportion of their market and over half of the used-car buyers—women. Women traditionally have not responded to technological advertising and marketing, whether it was technobabble or well done. The car that used to be most closely identified with woman-as-buyer (as opposed to woman-as-driver)—GM's Saturn—never mentions technology in its advertisements. The automobile market was changing rapidly in the late 1990s; women accounted for 60 percent of new car purchases by those under age twenty-five years and approximately 50 percent by those in the twenty-six- to forty-four-year age bracket (Widgery and McGaugh, 1992, 1993). The 1997 Bruskin-Goldring survey bore these numbers out. Widgery and McGaugh (1992, 1993) also found that there were gender differences in advertising appeals, although in the under-twenty-five-year age group the differences were not significant; women were more interested in dealer attributes than in product attributes than were men. If new car manufacturers were missing their market, however, they were light-years ahead of used-car sellers in their advertising.

We had had enough of a hint through our secondary research that women were buying more cars—both new and used—that one of the areas that we asked Bruskin-Goldring to investigate was gender differences in car purchasing. Women expect car dealers to be more trustworthy than men do, as well as to be more customer-service oriented and more flexible with pricing and trade-in allowances. They would like to see no-haggle pricing. Their expectations are not being met in terms of trustworthiness or customer-service orientation; otherwise, they felt that their expectations of the dealerships are being met. In terms of the features, women place a greater emphasis on a car's ride and handling, comfort and convenience, and safety and reliability, including warranties, than do men. As might be expected in a country that is as obsessed with its cars as is the United States, satisfaction with the cars purchased and their features is very high.

In June 1997, I attended the Marketing to Women Conference in New York; there were to be several speakers on how to market cars to women, in addition to sessions on marketing to women in general and across several product categories. For two days, speaker after speaker talked about a "new" market for selling cars to women and quoted statistics to bolster this statement. First was that women were buying about 50 percent of new cars in 1997, headed for 60 percent by 2005, and that they influenced 80 percent of new-car buying decisions; there was never a source or an attribution attached to these numbers, which I found high at the time and still do. I thought at the time that this statistic was probably that for women in the twenty-five- to forty-year age group, in which the percentage of working women is high, half of those buying new cars being women.

Second, the speakers stated that women buyers were overrepresented for several kinds of cars: compacts and subcompacts, near-luxury, sport-utility vehicles (SUVs, a relatively new kind of car at the time), and minivans. Many speakers felt that this overrepresentation was the result of the lifestage that these women were in rather than their preference. If one has elementary-school kids, one needs a vehicle with room for their soccer team, skates, bicycles, lots of groceries, and so forth. A two-seater is not practical at this point in a woman's life, even if what she really wants is a Mazda Miata (which was identified as the women's "midlife-crisis car"). Affluent women aged twenty-five to thirty-five years were buying luxury cars, the expensive SUVs, and minivans. The feeling of the speakers was that the women in that demographic would buy quite different cars when their family responsibilities changed as they and their families aged.

Women were seen as voracious information seekers and savvy shoppers. Their car-buying experience was small, so they tended to want even more information than usual. However (and this sounded much like the results of the American LIVES [1991] study, substituting "women" for "upscale buyers"), the information they got in the car market did not match the kinds of information available to them for other product categories. As a key example, the new-car advertisements, especially those on television, did not appeal to them so they did not even register with many women. More nontraditional media would be crucial for advertising cars to women; one of the best nontraditional media at the time was thought to be event sponsorship. Nevertheless, media containing product information would be needed to fill the gaps that women felt existed.

More than anything, women wanted respect (which they defined as being treated as the buyer, the decision maker, and not merely as an appendage) in the automobile-buying process, from the manufacturer and the dealer—and they overwhelmingly felt that they were not getting any respect. Interestingly, research seemed to indicate that although women felt that they were getting little respect on the showroom floor, certainly in contrast to men, both men and women now equally report being mistreated in the service experience because men no longer understand how a car works, given the new automotive and computer technology aboard.

Probably the most important theme at the conference, however, was the fact that, for any given car model, the psychographics and demographics of the women buyers were very much like those of the male buyers. In other words, the woman buyer of a Lexus looked much like the male buyer of a Lexus, much more so than did the female buyer of a Plymouth Voyager. Detroit has spent literally millions upon millions of dollars marketing cars to specific psychographic and demographic segments; it should be relatively easy to see that changing the gender of the buyer should not have a major impact on the psychographic segmentation of the car.

Having said this, however, some characteristics seem to track across the female car-buying experience, where women are more like other women. First, they are much less interested in product attributes than in the benefits that fit their needs of using the product; this trait carries over to other technical products that women buy. Women are much more interested than men in what the product will do for them than in what it consists of, e.g., how many megabytes of RAM are in the computer or how many horsepower are under the hood. Second, women need more specific information before making decisions than men do. This may be because men "know" what a car is and does and women do not; however, I think it has more to do with women's trying to understand the differences between cars (something that is certainly not intuitive) and to determine which one fits what they will do with their car—the analogue of "house types" in real estate. Third, women are more often presold when the go to the showroom than are men; it is then up to the dealer to complete the sale. Fourth, and more difficult to deal with, is the fact that most of the speakers at the conference felt that women do not want to be blatantly targeted. When called on this point and asked what they meant by "blatantly," the speakers retreated to the old story of the 1955 Dodge LeFemme, a pink and white car that came with color-coordinated "female accessories."

Although the car speakers focused on new cars, there was some information available about used cars. The psychographics of the car tend to go with the car as it ages, within certain parameters; it is the demographics that change. Most of the conferees with whom I discussed the matter seemed to feel that the "new" used-car market was too new to make pronouncements about, but they felt that the two-year-old car selling for $15,000 and up (the core of the Bruskin-Goldring [1997] research) would attract people more like new-car buyers than the traditional used-car buyer. This would certainly bring women into the used-car equation for the first time in a big way; it is no secret that women were not a big proportion of the used-car market, although a bigger proportion of the "dealer" used-car market than the used-car market as a whole.

The upshot of the conference seemed to be that marketing cars to women was becoming more like marketing cars to men, with the difference that women want and need more information and they will go to great lengths to obtain it—and need to because the traditional information sources were not satisfying their needs. Making the information-gathering process easier and more complete should benefit anyone who manages to achieve it. Again, this conclusion duplicates the findings about information-gathering in the American LIVES (1991) study.

The secondary research and the Bruskin-Goldring (1997) research, when added to the Marketing to Women Conference, led us at DCI to conclude that it was going to be quite possible to specifically target women buyers of used cars. We had discovered that women prioritized features quite differently from men, read advertisements differently, reacted to dealers and individual used-car sellers differently. In short, simply by segmenting on the single demographic of gender, it would be possible to create a whole new approach to used-car marketing. However, corporate imperatives intervened, and AutoAd had to be placed into the development deep-freeze again, as lack of funds and the needs of the real estate program dominated everyone's attention.

It was not until 2002 that AutoAd again received serious consideration, primarily because newspaper publishers who were using the real estate program were searching for more benefits from their investment in software. The conceptual leap from houses to cars is short for those who are primarily involved with classified advertising (and, in fact, the leap from houses and cars to death notices seems to be short, as several publishers who use the real estate programs have asked if it would be possible to automate the production of death notices). Although the research that had come before certainly informed the thoughts and design of the revived AutoAd, many things had changed. First, the ads were going to be more like the ads currently being produced than formerly thought appropriate with a program that can write well. Second, the World Wide Web had become a sales and advertising medium of choice, so the needs of the Web had to be taken into serious consideration in any program designed to utilize information search by consumers. Third, the search for a vehicle identification number (VIN) decoder was finally shelved.[1] Fourth, and probably most important, the decision had been made to use the Tribes as the segmentation scheme.

The latter decision, of course, should never have been made and, in a perfect world, would not have. However, there were substantial business reasons why it was—most having to do with the cost of performing another segmentation analysis and the time required, for AutoAd seemed to be needed relatively quickly. These "substantial business reasons" explain a lot of my disagreement with the Morgan and Levy (2002) assertion that every product or service should have its own segmentation scheme: a thought lovely in theory, but muddy in application. When a firm offers multiple products, there is always going to be the need (or temptation) to apply management attention and resources—and certainly at the very senior levels of management—across those lines. One of the resources will be the segmentation scheme; it would be extremely confusing and expensive to have one scheme for toothpaste and another for, say, soap, much less if the firm sold toothpaste and lawn service. VALS or PRIZM, or some other "grand scheme"—such as the Tribes—serves far better to maintain consistency in approach and communication across all the products offered by such a multiline firm. Belongers, in the VALS segmentation, buy toothpaste *and* soap; with a bit of exploration, one can discern patterns of consumption across both product lines in a single firm. Similarly, although Belongers rarely buy lawn service, Achievers do—and toothpaste. Of course, it is possible that the different products would be aimed at different segments; the firm might make toothpaste aimed at Belongers and soap aimed at Authenticks and a lawn service aimed at Achievers, but at least management would understand those two segments without having to learn a whole new corporate language by adopting an additional scheme.

The problem with using the Tribes to segment cars was that it was derived from a study whose respondents were in the market to buy or sell a single-family house, not cars. This was not a problem when the service was advertising for single-family houses. When applied to advertising for cars, entire populations were missed—populations that were important in the market for used cars. The bottom of that market probably does not often buy or sell houses; the Tribes scheme does not adequately address this segment, in my opinion. Approximately one-third of the U.S. population lives in rental housing and is therefore entirely ignored; this is a major portion of the market for used cars, and the needs and wants of this group are unknown and unknowable in the Tribes scheme. To remedy this defect, perceptual mapping was used to get a feel for where the different Tribes would buy different cars.[2]

Our research indicates that the Tribes to which the new-car manufacturers aim their models may not be the same Tribes that buy them used, which makes sense, particularly when Winners are concerned. Nevertheless, the American LIVES scheme (Lifestyle, Interests, Values, Expectations, and Symbols) would hold as a means for segmenting cars. Sukhdial et al. (1995) discuss the importance of values in segmenting cars, at least in the luxury segment (and, in truth, for most kinds of cars). Punj and Staelin (1983) have constructed a model for information search that explicitly encompasses prior information in the search process, including prior knowledge and prior memories of other decisions. Srinivasan and Ratchford (1991) include in their model a test of the buyer's belief structure. Morgan and Levy (2002) segment the car market differently from the Tribes, but they use attitude and behavior measures to do so. Farley et al. (1978) explore attitude formation and attitude change as they apply to types and models of cars. This last is important as I write this near the end of 2004 with gasoline prices at or near $2.00 per gallon for unleaded regular, and again in 2006 with gas around $2.80, forcing many people to consider mileage per gallon as a variable in their car-buying decision-making process, making gas-electric "hybrid" cars such as Toyota's Prius hot sellers and hurting sales of large SUVs, and placing the issue of incentives and gasoline prices squarely into the presidential campaign. By typing cars according to LIVES and being able to figure which gender would be more likely to buy, AutoAd contains a powerful method for writing advertisements that would make people want to consider the cars for which it was used to write ads.

Morgan and Levy (2002) target their book to marketers aiming at Baby Boomers—those people born between 1946 and 1964—and their elders. Understanding how this age group will react to physical and psychological changes over the next decade will be crucial to car manufacturers (and others). This group accounts for 67 percent of licensed drivers and will continue to account for the vast majority of new-car sales (Morgan and Levy, 2002, p. 319). Furthermore, given the realities of the economic climate and the findings of the Bruskin-Goldring research, this segment will continue to have a major impact on used-car sales. My father bought a used car for his last car purchase after buying nothing but new cars for forty years; he refused to pay more for a new car than he had paid for his first house despite the fact that his economic situation would have made it possible for him to do so. It is clear that simple segmentation by age is going to be difficult, although there are clearly cars that will not appeal to older drivers for a number of reasons, some physical and some emotional.

REVIEW QUESTIONS

1. What kind of car do you drive (make/model/year)? Compare it with the cars of the rest of the class. What does this list show?
2. What kind of car(s) do your parent(s) drive? Compare them with the cars of the parents of the rest of the class. What does this list show?
3. Compare and contrast the two lists. Beyond income levels between parents and college students, why might there be differences in the lists?

Chapter 15

Food

How many consumption items resonate more with autobiographical memories than food? In so many ways food is more than simply fuel to get our bodies through the day. There are many cultural splits in food: rice, potatoes, corn, or wheat for your starch? Oil or butter for your fat? Fish or meat or beans for your protein? These splits can be plotted on world maps and are centuries—in many cases, millennia—old. There are even splits in as new a country as the United States. Fischer (1989) draws lines that divide foodways here and mark someone's birth area. Regular consumption of cornmeal, pork, and boiled greens mark people as Southern as much as their accent, even though this trilogy of food was present on the entire eighteenth-century frontier for economic reasons. Regular consumption of wheat bread, beef, and cold salad marks the northerner. Pie for breakfast, while sometimes thought to mark the true New England Yankee, was as recently as the 1930s a sign of someone who had spent significant time on a farm where breakfast had not yet been reached by Graham's "reform" from eggs and meat and dessert to cereal and juice.

Jeffrey Steingarten was appointed food critic of *Vogue* magazine in 1989, but he was concerned about his ability to fulfill the post.

> I, like everybody I knew, suffered from a set of powerful, arbitrary, and debilitating attractions and aversions at mealtime. I feared that I could be no more objective than an art critic who detests the color yellow or suffers from red-green color blindness. . . . Suddenly, intense food preferences, whether phobias or cravings, struck me as the most serious of all personal limitations. That very day I sketched out a Six-Step Program to liberate my palate and my soul. No smells or tastes are innately repulsive, I assured myself, and what's learned can be forgot.

He then proceeded to make himself a list of his food phobias.

1. Foods I wouldn't touch even if I were starving on a desert island. None, except maybe insects. Many cultures find insects highly nutritious and love their crunchy texture. . . . [No] innate human programming keeps me from eating them, too.
2. Foods I wouldn't touch even if I were starving on a desert island until absolutely everything else runs out.
3. Foods I might eat if I were starving on a desert island but only if the refrigerator were filled with nothing but chutney, sea urchin, and felafel [which he had put in under #2 above].

He then immersed himself in the scientific literature on human food selection and discovered that

> by design and by destiny, humans are omnivores. Our teeth and digestive systems are all-purpose and ready for anything. Our genes do not dictate what foods we should find tasty or repulsive. We come into the world with a yen for sweets . . . and a weak aversion to bitterness, and after four months develop a fondness for salt. Some people are born particularly sensitive to one taste or odor; others have trouble digesting milk sugar or wheat gluten. . . . All human cultures consider fur, paper, and hair inappropriate as food. . . . And that's about it. Everything else is *learned.* Newborns are not repelled even by the sight and smell of putrefied meat crawling with maggots. . . . Yet by the age of twelve, we all suffer from a haphazard collection of food aversions ranging from revulsion to indifference. (Steingarten, 1997, pp. 3-8)

Our food preferences, our "foodways," are learned—and therefore are cultural and thus subject to segmentation along psychographic lines. American children are notorious for preferring foods that are solo, not touching other foods,[1] and fairly dry; this set of criteria is unlikely to be universal unless one also discovers that Thai children or Cantonese Chinese children also insist on being served their food like this. The learned, cultural aspect of our foodways also has a profound impact on food relief attempts; people who are used to eating rice have a difficult time dealing with flour—if for no other reason than that they have little or no idea what to do with a bag of flour.

Some of the differences are climatic—national cuisines tend to be rice *or* wheat *or* corn, butter *or* oil. Furthermore, despite the large Columbian Exchange, by which New World natives such as tomatoes, potatoes, maize, and squash migrated to the Old World and the Old World staples of wheat, rice, cattle, sheep, and pigs were brought to the New World, deep down much of the age-old foodways remain basically unchanged.

Beyond the impact of food on our bodies as fuel, food bears a substantial symbolic component. Not only are bread and wine sacramental in the Christian churches (symbolizing—or becoming—the body and blood of Jesus as sacrifice), various foods and beverages become more freighted with symbol than with nutrition over time. The bagel and lox combination (Regelson, 1981), the bottomless cup of coffee (Taylor, 1981)—made almost iconic by Garrison Keillor in episode after episode of *The News from Lake Woebegone* in his *Prairie Home Companion* radio show and other shows he has hosted—the "religious" nature of the health food movement (Dubisch, 1981) all have been examined by anthropologists with the intent of discovering the "why" of the "what," the symbolism packed inside the product.

Of course, part of the symbolism of the product is the product itself. Although one may buy the same brand in similar packaging with similar advertising around the world, the product itself may be different because of local tastes, conditions, or regulations (Ball et al., 2004). Large producers are trying to move in the direction of standardization; government regulators around the world are heading in the same direction as well. Differences remain worldwide, of course, differences in manufacturing, differences in water, differences in climate. Nevertheless, foodways worldwide are converging, albeit slowly (Ball et al., 2004).

The largest part of the Columbian Exchange, of course, was people—at least in the exchange from the Old World to the New. The first of the immigrants to what is now the United States—"Albion's Seed" in Fischer's (1989) title—were the English and Scots-Irish. They brought the basics and the animals with them, and to a large extent at the beginning, the New World had little impact on them and their eating, leading to the universal colonial "starving times" as immigrants tried to continue to cook and eat exactly as they had at home in the face of crop failures. It was not until the colonists began to adapt to what the New World offered, especially corn and beans, that they found abundance; foods could be grown in such quantity that want all but disappeared in what has become the United States in the seventeenth century—except for economic reasons. This abundance became the basis early on for rejoicing and for the religious celebration of the English "Harvest Home" celebration—Thanksgiving.

Thanksgiving, of course, is a major part of the American foundation myth. Who among us has not heard of the First Thanksgiving at Plymouth, when the Pilgrims invited the Indians to partake in the bounteous harvest? Immediately our founding myth starts to have difficulties in the face of reality. Many, many cultures have harvest festivals; they usually occur around harvest time—which in New England would be October, not "the fourth Thursday in November." It is highly unlikely that the menu encompassed the "standard" Thanksgiving fare of turkey and sweet potatoes; we do know about venison (the Indians brought it), corn would be obvious (it was a harvest festival, after all, and the Indians had shown the Pilgrims how to grow corn)—otherwise, it would probably have been a fairly standard Eastern England meal with the addition of several New World items.

Thanksgiving is the one day of the year when we "know" what everyone is eating; we merely do not know when they are sitting down. "Thanksgiving is a collective ritual that celebrates material abundance enacted through feasting" (Wallendorf and Arnould, 1991, p. 13). "Everyone" eats turkey, stuffing of some kind, both white and sweet potatoes, cranberries in some form, and pumpkin pie. Whether this is, in fact, true is less important than the fact that part of the American myth is that they are; Thanksgiving Day is seen by many people in the United States as being the same for everyone. Furthermore, because the meal and the day have remained unchanged over the years, we are participating in an unchanged ritual (Rook, 1985).

Much of the myth is actually buttressed by fact. Wallendorf and Arnould (1991) report that turkey was eaten by all of the people in their sample; Steingarten (1997) concurs. The other important point that Wallendorf and Arnould (1991, p. 23) make is that, beyond the anchors of the meal, the "details of the meals reflect differences regarded as traditions by particular families." Most families seem to have one or more idiosyncratic items that have graced their Thanksgiving tables for years if not generations; it would not be a "real" Thanksgiving for that family without their appearance. Thus, there is a merging of American tradition with family traditions, and, like the national myth, so too are family myths distorted from reality over time. Reference to "always" seems to go no further back than the grandparents' generation and rarely allows for the fact that most families are a blend of several strands of traditions as husbands and wives over successive generations have come to terms with which sets of traditions will be adopted or how two sets of traditions—or, in this era of blended families, several sets of traditions—will be merged.

Furthermore, Thanksgiving Day has changed over the years. At first, it was a New England holiday; it as not celebrated nationally until during the Civil War, when Abraham Lincoln declared it. As recently as the 1930s it was the often the last Thursday in November until the last Thursday was the fifth Thursday and Franklin Roosevelt was urged to move it to the fourth Thursday to make a longer Christmas shopping season during the Depression. At one time there was a much larger religious component; religious observances of the day now are mostly private and family centered. Of course, the food itself has also changed. As branded and prepared foods have become available, they have appeared as part of the meal, sometimes as a seamless substitute (Butterball turkey for one from the local butcher, for instance), sometimes as a de novo introduction (Jell-O gelatin for a fruit salad, as an example).

Wallendorf and Arnould (1991) make several claims about Thanksgiving and their study of it in terms of a better understanding of family and tradition and of the roles that each plays in our consumption of food as more than fuel. It is clear that Thanksgiving has become a family-oriented celebration of material abundance and of the more general consumer culture. One of their final claims is that through the use of branded food products on an ongoing basis, people are able to create "little traditions" that can be as meaningful and durable as any others in the family history (1991, p. 29).

Many other family stories tend to involve food, frequently quite symbolically (see Reichl [1998, 2001] for almost endless examples of family stories by a food writer who comes from a background in which food had many uses—fuel for the body was almost unthought of in her childhood). Many think that it is mostly "ethnic" families, particularly those of Jewish or Italian extraction, that have the stories in which food plays such a symbolic role. Watchers of the television show *The Sopranos* or the movies in the *Godfather* series frequently remark that everything seems to happen around a table. Perhaps this is less ethnic than social class. It is, after all, a truism of American literature that the big family table in the kitchen is the mainstay, the stage on which so many things about the family are discussed; food may be eaten, but it is the kitchen table as the center of the home (rather than the house) that is the setting, and what is on the table is of much less importance. In large measure, this is an outdated view. The kitchen table has been replaced by the family room and the discussions around the table by the family watching the television—and yet, this view is probably superceded itself in the twenty-first century by individuals, each eating in a separate room often at different times, and watching television or videos or using the Internet.

The family as a unit has changed into the family as a collection of individuals through three generations, as the blue-collar, highly ethnic families of the American literature view have been replaced first by blue/pink/first-generation-white collars away from "the old neighborhoods," no longer in rust-belt cities, but more and more in the Sunbelt, and then in the current generation by "knowledge workers," with both parents working long hours out of the house, spending more and more time commuting to more and more distant jobs, and food being pulled out of the freezer or bought at the supermarket's "ready-to-eat" counter and nuked as people wander in and out of the kitchen as their schedules allow. The Norman Rockwell painting of Thanksgiving dinner at Grandma's with which everyone is familiar is so old-fashioned as to no longer be quaint; it is noncongruent with everyday life for a large and growing proportion of the population.

In part of the introductory essay to *The Consumer Society Reader* (Schor and Holt, 2000), Holt and Schor (2000, p. xvii) discuss the triumph of consumption over production, labeling it "consuming as liberation." This is seemingly true with food, in particular, as food preparation in the home for the family has long been seen as a form of drudgery by many women, and advertisers and television show writers have long made working in the kitchen seem to be the antithesis of modern womanhood. This has gone from being a tenet of women's liberation and feminist critique to a cultural truth that seems to apply to both genders. The Boy Scouts of America used to require the Cooking Merit Badge in order for a Scout to become an Eagle; the requirement has been dropped.[2] School systems that still require cooking classes in middle school have become fairly uncommon; those that do, of course, require it for both boys and girls. In many cases, however, the curriculum has been reduced to little more than how to open cans and microwave prepared foods. It has become an article of faith that the family has changed so much in the past generation that cooking on an everyday basis for a family that sits down together at the same time is almost impossible.

This change in the family, of course, leaves a marvelous set of lifestyle approaches to segmentation. Because some families still are nuclear, with one parent staying at home full or part time, it would be possible to make food that would appeal to the "maternal" in the food preparer (usually the female in this segment), seeking to have her buy foods with little processed content or that would require more exten sive preparation. An example of a product for this segment would be a cake mix that would require the addition of eggs, water, and oil and a significant amount of time to mix the batter. Another segment would be for a family in which the parents (or a single parent) both work out of the house and the children are off in different directions. The cake mix for this segment would require only the addition of water, but it would still need to be mixed and stuck into a traditional oven. For the segment in which no one is home and nothing is cooked from scratch, the product could be shelf-stable batter that is mixed and in a microwaveable pan already, needing merely to be placed into the microwave for a minute or two.

However, this segmentation scheme treats food as fuel more than anything else and ignores all of the other components that food and eating carry. Because eating is one of the basic needs of life—and yet gluttony is one of the Seven Deadly Sins—we need to examine some of the other freight. Desire is part of the baggage that studies of consumption often forget to pack (Belk et al., 2000). Giving in to desire is seen as a loss of control, and yet eating food that we do not desire is problematic both as a denial of our culture and nurture (Steingarten, 1997) and as a means for ignoring what our body is telling us about not eating, with all of the dangers of obesity inherent in eating when we no longer need or want to. Nevertheless, "giving in" to desire is very close to a descent into the "lower order" of the physical body and not climbing into our "higher and better natures" as beings who are not dependent on our minds (Belk et al., 2000).

Although the rise of Romanticism in the eighteenth and nineteenth centuries removed much of the stigma associated with the body in the mind-body dichotomy at the same time that it allowed for an increase in the social acceptability of the continuing desire for goods (Campbell, 1987, 1997), the stigma has not totally disappeared. We in the United States still bear the weight of the failed experiment of Prohibition and the impetus that caused the politicization of a particular kind of consumption, and the fact that the experiment failed has in no way lessened the impetus to repeat it for other commodities in hopes that *this* time prohibiting consumption that one group or another does not approve of will work. Much of the nutritional information that appears in the various media in waves of information, denial, and retraction or amendment seems almost more driven by morality than science. If certain foods are bad for people, one is always looking for a group attempting to make them illegal to sell (on the Prohibition model) instead of moving them into a different plane on the Food and Drug Administration's food pyramid. As I write this in August 2004, there is a craze for low-carbohydrate foods (to the extent of developing low-carbohydrate ice cream, low-carbohydrate bread, and low-carbohydrate taco shells), as one form or another of the Atkins Diet sweeps the newspapers and magazines as the silver bullet to clean out America's arteries from the accumulations of plaque that has built up—mostly caused by the meat-rich American diet—threatening to choke our nation's coronary arteries.

It is unlikely, then, that such a straight-on segmentation as described for cake mixes will work, and it is unlikely that other simplistic segmentation schemes will either. There are certain fault lines that run through the larger American culture that give hints on how such segmentation schemes might look, beyond hoping that some larger scheme such as VALS or PRIZM might be able to do the job based on psychodemographics.

One of these tectonic plates is that based on ethnic distinctions. First-generation Americans have long clustered into "Little Italies," "Little Saigons," or "Little Havanas," where members of the same ethnic group owned stores that sold products available from the home country, where newspapers in the home language (whether from the home country or produced in the United States) continued to support the original culture, where churches and other houses of worship could conduct services in the home language. Within a generation or two these enclaves had shrunk in size and the children and grandchildren had become "hyphenated Americans," but many of the cultural support institutions were still in place and important, particularly the stores and restaurants that now sold what for most of their customers was "grandma's food." The daily meals had probably become mostly American, but for special days the old-country foods were still important. If American streets turned out not to be paved with gold, the American diet had also served as a beacon of hope, with its huge quantities of meat and white bread—which for millions of European peasants served as markers of economic success.

Segmentation of food based on ethnicity would be possible; in fact, it has been practiced for years. If we are serious about continuing to practice psychographic segmentation, however, then simple ethnicity—a basic demographic item—will not do. There is also no reason to stop with ethnicity, trying to find all the German Americans to sell them sauerkraut, for instance. If the United States never truly became the melting pot of legend, its food choices have. Although Fischer (1989) states that the underlying food choices we make are reflective of the original settlement patterns, there is a significant overlay of other choices. There are significant psychographic reasons why a family would stay with the original foodways, serving Southern food seven days a week, for instance. However, others have significant psychographic reasons to adopt and adapt a whole variety of other food choices, mixing and matching among a wide variety of dishes from other ethnic groups, sometimes on the same table. It is now quite possible to go to a supermarket in a relatively small market and buy prepackaged Mexican food, Chinese food, Thai food, and many others. The people who cook these foods are segmentable from those who do not—they are different psychographically, they are reachable through various media (and were before the introduction of cable television's Food Network), and there are enough of them to be worth reaching.

A second tectonic plate is vegetarianism versus meat eating. There is a dizzying variety of vegetarianism, from veganism—in which the strict practitioners not only abstain from eating animal products of any sort but refuse to wear clothing items from animals, abjuring leather shoes for cloth or synthetic—through those who eat dairy and eggs, to those who basically abstain from red meat. I do not wish to get into a debate about which vegetarianism is the "true" one here, simply to state that each state along the continuum is potentially psychographically segmentable from each of the others. In the absence of a religious reason, the various vegetarianisms are lifestyle options that people have voluntarily chosen to follow; therefore, as different market segments they are more similar to each other than they are to the "normal" American diet. However, any food product that faces the market as two segments—vegetarian versus meat-eating—is going to face difficulties as the various factions in the vegetarian community debate each other about the value of their diet.

Overall, the number of Americans who say they are vegetarian varies between 1 and 6 percent depending on how the question was asked, who was doing the surveying, and when the survey was taken; however, even the lowest number is over 2 million nationally, a figure that seems quite low today. If one adds the number of people who eat a meatless meal once a week or occasionally to the mix, it is clear that this is now a viable market to reach. It is also a market that is in need of food information unlike others, because there are so many dos and don'ts to making a vegetarian menu nutritious. Nevertheless, it is clear that vegetarianism has come out of the health-food-store culture and is now more comfortably mainstream.

Another tectonic plate is the "healthy-food" market. This is the group that I would define by saying that they are trying to get away from the "basic American diet" of too much meat and other saturated fat sources and to increase the amount of fiber they eat—not to become vegetarians, nor because they dislike the foods they are giving up, but because to do so would reduce their risks of heart disease and certain kinds of cancer. These consumers are "defining good food negatively by a logic of risk avoidance . . . to avoid the bad . . . [foods]" (Ostberg, 2002). This group is of uncertain size if for no other reason than, given human nature, people do not want to admit that they are eating foods they do not really want to eat to avoid dying early. The consumers will couch their food statements more positively by stating that it is "healthier" or claim that their doctor has told them to restrict this or that item from their diet, and the more they have deviated from their previous diet, the more they will tend to blame doctors, dieticians, and the government for their plight. Nevertheless, it is quite clear that this market segment is large and growing and in desperate need of further information. One of the more interesting possibilities is that these are the same people that the American LIVES (1991) study found are crying out for more and better information in residential real estate classified advertisements and that Morgan and Levy (2002) found want more information in various other categories—people who are mostly Baby Boomers, mostly higher income, who are used to having information provided to them by people who want them to buy their goods and services.

Morgan and Levy (1993, 2002) found that this segment, which they call "Nutrition Concerned," is the largest of their three segments for all Baby Boom groups. They are "committed to eating fresh fruits and vegetables and cutting back on their salt intake." These goals have been suggested to them by their doctors as well as by their information gathering (Morgan and Levy, 1993:296). Far more than others, "[the] Nutrition Concerned are focused on avoiding fats and eating enough fiber." They work to reach these goals by "reading labels before trying new food products" and are the only segment "committed to label reading" (pp. 139-140). There are many media outlets that will enable a marketer who wants to reach this group to be able to. The most intriguing comment in Morgan and Levy's list is the label reading; these people do seem to be information seekers. If ecologically conscious consumer behavior is more effectively explained by psychographics than by demographics, as Straughan and Roberts (1999) state, would nutrition consciousness likewise be more effectively explained by psychographics? Probably.

In the Tribes segmentation, the group that Straughan and Roberts describe and that Morgan and Levy describe is the Authenticks (the Societally Conscious in VALS), not the Winners (Achievers). SRI International (1983) produced a video of couples in each of three of their segments (Societally Conscious, Achievers, and Belongers) talking about various products that they used and why. The Societally Conscious couple talked about two of their products in nutritional and ecological terms. The food product was a large carboy of olive oil, produced down the road from them—low transportation costs, low ecological impact because of the size of the container and the fact that they presented the same container for refilling, and nutritional because it was olive oil. A key point of interest is that this video is now twenty years old and the Baby Boom cohort is now starting to approach sixty years of age, "seniors" in name and in health problems. Even Winners, who typically have sneered at the whole-grain and vegetables approach to diet that so many Societally Conscious consumers worked toward for various reasons, are now faced with elevated cholesterol counts and the specter of colorectal cancer—and their doctors are advocating higher intakes of fiber and lower intakes of saturated fats. That the demographic is similar and that the diets are converging should not mask the fact that they are doing so from quite different motivations.

The overarching consideration, and one that will be solved psycho-graphically, is that both the Winners and Authenticks across this divide need and want nutritional and other food information. However, the two groups seek out different information differently and process it quite differently. Winners do not want to read much; large blocks of text turn them off cold. Winners are the quintessential users of bullet-pointed information. They want short, quick, and punchy. Authenticks, on the other hand, are quite willing—even eager—to read large blocks of very dense text. Nutritional information on boxes and other food packages is only the beginning for them rather than the total of the information about their products that Authenticks will consume. We found the same difference in information needs and processing styles when we looked at Authenticks and Winners with respect to real estate advertising (Cahill and Polansky, 1997), and we have continued to find the same split as we work through various other items with the Tribes.[3] It will thus behoove any food marketer to undertake two quite different information campaigns if they want to serve both sides of this information dichotomy in their segmentation scheme.

The last of the tectonic plates that I wish to discuss here is eating at home versus eating out; the operative word here is "eating." There is a large amount of food bought "ready to eat" or "needing only to be heated"; the food is fully prepared for take away from grocery stores, "restaurants" (I am not quite sure what to call Boston Market, which is almost prototypical of this type of store), and other venues. Always available in large cities—the New York delicatessens have always served this market well, as have other similar venues that have sold large quantities of "take out" for years—this category of food is now available nationwide. I do not include here the large amount of fast food consumed off premises nor pizza delivered to the home. I am rather referring to what one might delicately call "real food" or "full meals," meals that include the more-traditional American setting of meat and starch and vegetable and dessert—or its equivalents from other cuisines or other options (such as fish instead of the meat). Part of the eating-out experience has always been the fact that the cook at home does not have to cook at home when the family goes to a restaurant; the new reality is that the cook at home does not have to cook at home any more; someone can stop at the grocery store or at Boston Market or the equivalent and bring home a meal that is as nutritious as one prepared at home. The trade-off, of course, is that these purchased meals are more expensive, but the family gains time and the cook at home gains a lot of time. There are several potential approaches to marketing the nutritional value of these meals while de-emphasizing the convenience (their big selling point currently) and making the family feel that it is all right nutritionally to buy these meals that they already want to buy because of convenience.

Many years ago, I was involved in a series of focus groups in the South for one of the spiral-sliced ham companies. We were trying to find out how the buyers used their hams and why the recently implemented sandwich deli in the stores was not reaching sales projections. Not surprisingly, the hams were primarily bought for an occasion, such as Easter or Thanksgiving, when a large number of people were expected in the house and the cook wanted to be with her guests (all the focus group participants were female). Somewhat surprisingly, the second-biggest use for the hams was for the women to take as a bereavement contribution when they went to visit a family who had just had a death; again, the size of the ham made it an obvious choice when faced with large numbers of people and to give as a gift. The sandwiches available did not appeal to the participants because they were already looking to use up a large quantity of ham in the house. Rather than a sandwich, they would have preferred to have quarter-hams available so that they could have this ham that they loved and viewed as a supremely premium product at other times of the year, for nonoccasions. The company has since repositioned the delis for people who are looking for a lunch and have added smaller portions (with the bone in or out) for take away.

Morgan and Levy (2002) call for "motivational segmentation" to move Americans to "better" eating habits, as defined by various governmental and nongovernmental agencies. Although I am not quite sure what "motivational segmentation" might be that differentiates it from behavioral or attitudinal segmentation, it does seem to be a somewhat Big Brother approach to people whose eating habits put them at risk for heart disease, diabetes, and other conditions that worsen as one ages. Although this may seem somewhat dictatorial, Morgan and Levy present statistics that show that eating habits that deviate significantly from the nutritional guidelines of the governmental and nongovernmental agencies lead to higher societal health care costs; as the population in the West and in the United States in particular gets older, the cumulative effect of bad eating habits since childhood will inexorably lead to more serious health concerns and higher health care costs. President Clinton's quadruple coronary-bypass operation probably cannot be solely attributed to the infamous McDonald's restaurant in Little Rock, Arkansas, where he used to stop to eat after he jogged—but his well-known fondness for Big Macs cannot have helped his coronary health.

REVIEW QUESTIONS

1. List the food you have for Thanksgiving dinner. When and where do you eat this dinner? Alone with your immediate family or with an extended family? What other rituals for the holiday do you follow?
2. Compare your answers in Question 1 with those of the rest of the class. Where are there areas of similarity? Difference? How comfortable would you be exchanging places on Thanksgiving Day with another member of your class? Why or why not?
3. List the foods you have for the main meal on July 4th. When and where do you eat this meal? How comfortable would you be in exchanging places with a classmate on July 4th?
4. Why do you think there are differences between the answers for Thanksgiving and July 4th?

Chapter 16

Health Care

Kaiser Permanente, the country's original health maintenance organization (HMO), is now marketing the fact that they are trying to get their members to practice healthy lifestyles. "We stand for broccoli, Pilates, and dental floss" (Rundle, 2004, p. B3). Of course, the original slant of the HMO was that prevention was less costly than treatment. Therefore, frequent "well-person" visits were going to be encouraged, vaccinations would be paid for, and health "counselors" would be available to meet with members to ensure that they stayed healthy—it would profit the HMO to do these things.

Morgan and Levy (1993, 2002) divide the health market for those aged forty years and over into four segments: Proactives, Faithful Patients, Optimists, and Disillusioned. The Proactives (33 percent of the total) are committed to exercising and eating right. They are convinced that their actions will have a positive effect on their health. They are intensely interested in obtaining all the information on their health that they can. They trust their doctors and respect the health care system, but they also have no difficulty prodding their doctors with information that they have found rather than waiting for the doctors to bring up the information. They are compliant patients who do what they are told and take their medications as directed. Faithful Patients (26 percent of the total) know what they should be doing to improve their health but admit that they fail to take those actions. They take no responsibility for their health and are apt to turn to doctors, pharmacists, and over-the-counter medications to help them get better; this segment is also prone to turn to religion in times of poor health. This segment is very interested in joining an HMO that would cover all of their health care needs.

Optimists believe they are in terrific health; this belief is fostered by good luck, great genes, or infrequent health examinations. They

doi:10.1300/5560_20

think that they rarely get sick, and, when they do get sick, they think that there was not much they could have done to have avoided it. Optimists (20 percent of the total) try to avoid taking prescription medications and see little need for health care delivered by an HMO. The Disillusioned's (21 percent of the total) greatest concern is having insufficient health insurance. They are highly critical of today's health care system and feel alienated from doctors. According to this segment, prescription medications are to be avoided if possible. One concern they have is that of harmful drug interactions. The Disillusioned would like to live a long life and act to improve their health. Their interest in achieving good health, however, is thwarted by their lack of access to health care and their reluctance to find information on their own.

I find the percentage of Proactives to be much higher than I would expect from talking with people and from general reading. In fact, Morgan and Levy (2002, p. 175) almost immediately begin to cast doubt on their own segment sizes with their statement that they found that "6 percent of the forty and older U.S. population practices all three of the positive behaviors": have a "correct" Body Mass Index (although how this is a behavior is beyond my comprehension), do not smoke, and exercise four or more times a week at an aerobic level. They then state that 4 percent of the forty and older population are obese, smoke, and do not exercise four times a week. The rest of the population falls between, with one or two negative behaviors—mostly obesity. If the Proactives are 33 percent of the population, and only 6 percent fit with all three of the healthful behaviors, I see a categorization and definitional problem, because it is well known and well publicized that the three behaviors do help keep one healthy. Morgan and Levy (2002) have similar problems with their numbers as they go through several different health issues. This is a major problem with resegmenting for every study; every study is different, and the results cannot be tied together to get a comprehensive and meaningful picture of the total reality of the population. In this case—the health care of the American population as it ages through the first half of the twenty-first century—this lack of any metatheory is an extremely critical failing. If, as Morgan and Levy (1993, p. 267) state, those over fifty years then represented 26 percent of the U.S. population but consumed 56 percent of all health-related products and services, it is obvious that this demographic segment is spending a huge amount on health care.

The National Institutes of Health (NIH) has started to take major actions to stem what it calls an epidemic of bad lifestyle choices that lead to major medical problems. Barbara Alving, Acting Director of the National Heart, Lung, and Blood Institute, sounded the alarm about a "striking" increase in hypertension over the past ten years in the adult population. Data from 1999-2000 showed that about 65 million adults had hypertension. This is an increase of 15 million individuals, 8 percentage points of proportion, from 1988-1994 data showing that only 50 million people had hypertension.

> The hypertension trend is not unexpected given the increase in obesity and an aging population. Obesity contributes to the development of hypertension and the current epidemic of overweight and obesity in the U.S. has set the stage for an increase in high blood pressure. We also know that high blood pressure becomes more common as people get older. At age 55, those who do not have high blood pressure have a 90 percent chance of developing it at some point in their lives. (Alving, 2004, p. 1)

The NIH Obesity Research Task Force reported a research plan in August 2004 (NIH, 2004). Their statement that obesity has risen to epidemic levels and leads to devastating and costly health problems and reduces life expectancy tracks with Alving's statement. They found obesity to be a strong risk factor for type 2 diabetes and heart disease; it is also a risk factor for some cancers and is associated with depression. The greatest increase in obesity over the past two decades have been in the prevalence of extreme obesity. "Left unabated, the escalating rates of obesity in the U.S. population will place a severe burden on the Nation's health and its healthcare system" (NIH, 2004, p. 1). The program includes research toward preventing and treating obesity through lifestyle modification such as exercise and diet, medical interventions such as drugs and surgery, and breaking the link between obesity and its associated health conditions. Furthermore, NIH has recognized that certain populations are disproportionately affected by obesity: African Americans, Hispanics, and Native Americans. Socioeconomic status is also related to obesity, which is more prevalent among the poor. It is possible that because of pregnancy and/or menopause women are more susceptible to obesity. Finally,

NIH recognizes that it is crucial in the face of this growing epidemic that research needs to be translated from the laboratory bench to the health care providers' toolkit as quickly as possible (NIH, 2004). Of course, the Morgan and Levy (2002) Proactives will be on top of the research and will not need the translational research that NIH is planning to do to take their other research to the bedside.

However, the bedside, in the hands of the doctors and allied health professionals, is clearly not the most important place for the results of this research. It is in the "hearts and minds" of every American adult, because it is their behaviors—in terms of both eating and exercising—that need to be changed, and the research that the NIH is starting must lead the way to that change by providing knowledge of the correct behaviors to follow. The age at which we need to start winning the hearts and minds grows younger and younger (Buss, 2004). An advisory panel recently issued its final recommendations for changing the food pyramid, reminding all that whole-grain bread is better than white, fruits and vegetables are necessary, and eating fewer calories is the only way to reduce weight (Dreyfus, 2004). These recommendations have been well known for some time, but— to quote my ex-mother-in-law—"my grandmother did not come to America to eat brown bread and beans." How to change minds and behavior becomes a crucial question.

Actually, it has been a crucial task for quite some time. As Mills (1988) stated,

> the prophets of an emergent super health-conscious generation are busily revising their estimates. For despite the fact that fewer Americans are relying solely on the traditional medical establishment . . . for their health care and are increasingly participating in the management of their own health[,]

this super-health-conscious generation did not emerge. Furthermore, "actual health behavior often contradicts measured attitudes and knowledge" (Mills, 1988, p. ES-1). This is an acknowledgment of the difficulty of changing ancestral foodways, among other items. During this study, VALS found that three broad aspects of participatory health emerged as the most meaningful and important to marketers: preventive medical strategies, choice of physicians and allied health professionals, and self-medication.

While discussing the Mills VALS report, one has to remember the publication date of 1988; it reads in many ways as though it was written the day before yesterday. Mills stated that the then-current status of Americans and preventive health could best be described as a wide disparity between knowledge and attitudes on the one hand and actions and behavior on the other. Exercise patterns had shown little change, despite increased purchases of sporting equipment—of course, purchases of sporting equipment are poor predictors of their use (see Table 16.1 for percentages of the VALS Types who exercise); we all know people who have rowing machines, treadmills, and so forth in their closets. Dietary habits reflected the current "bipolar food product offerings" of health-oriented foods on the one side and rich, high-fat, high-calorie on the other, and the low-carbohydrate craze of Atkins and South Beach are little help in this case. Orange juice consumption is down in 2004 because it is very high in fruit sugars despite the fact that it is also high in vitamin C and, if it is not strained, nonsoluble fiber, both positive attributes for other health crazes—but at the moment, it is the "low-carb" craze that is dominant.

Mills (1988) also examined the mechanisms by which the various VALS types examined the bewildering choices among physicians and allied health professionals and hospitals. He found that in many respects consumers chose their doctors and hospitals much as they did other consumer products—looking at positive and negative attributes of the products and services. "The traditional archetype of the physician as the infallible healer with unquestionable authority is no longer the desired combination of attributes" (p. 15). Most consumers seemed to want physicians to have a pleasing bedside manner. Beyond agreement on this general attribute, the VALS segments differed in their preferred physician characteristics: The Need-Driven and Outer-Directed placed "a great deal of importance on a physician's reputation, whereas the Inner-Directed prefer physicians with a holistic health orientation" (p. 16). This would come as no surprise to those who know the VALS typology and know the Outer-Directed's drive for status and outer appeal. With regard to health care facilities, the Need-Driven and Belongers find religious-affiliated hospitals most appealing, whereas Achievers and the Inner-Directed tend to look for university-affiliated teaching hospitals (Mills, 1988, p. ES-2).

TABLE 16.1. Individuals engaging in exercise programs.

Tribes	1982 (%)	1987 (%)
Inside the house		
United States total	15	14
Survivors	7	4
Sustainers	6	10
Belongers	9	8
Emulaters	19	17
Achievers	20	21
I-Am-Me's	20	24
Experientials	33	20
Societally Conscious	20	23
Outside the house		
United States total	19	17
Survivors	9	5
Sustainers	15	13
Belongers	12	11
Emulators	25	17
Achievers	22	22
I-Am-Me's	33	24
Experientials	37	22
Societally Conscious	26	29

Source: Mills, 1988, p. 6.

The third topic Mills's research addressed was the self-medication of Americans. Although this may sound like an extraordinarily modern topic, Americans have been notorious for self-medication for over two hundred years. Patent medicines flourished for decades that were full of tonics and alcohol and ingredients that were known at the time to be toxic.[1] However, Mills looked at more-reasoned medicine; the drive since the late 1980s has been to take medications from prescription to over-the-counter status, thus giving consumers greater choice in product selection. Information on self-medicating products has proliferated through different channels, such as newspapers, magazines, and television. The network evening news programs in the early twenty-first century seem to be sponsored exclusively by prescription drugs, some of which are poised to come off prescription status. Interestingly, despite the increase in sources of health information, most people considered the physician as their key source; Mills's research predates the massive amount of television advertising for prescription drugs, most of it designed to get consumers to ask their doctors to prescribe them the advertised medications for ailments that they need to tell their doctors that they have. The Societally Conscious, however, cited newspapers and magazine articles as their second-most used source, after doctors. They and the Experientials are the most open to accepting the efficacy of over-the-counter drugs that started out as prescription, and they, unlike other segments, favor store-brand products over the higher priced national brands (Mills, 1988, p. ES-2).

In the eighteen years since Mills's research, the population has aged and there has been increased spending on health care. The American Association of Retired Persons (AARP) commissioned Roper Starch Worldwide to field a large survey in 1998 on the subject of the Baby Boomers and their retirement (AARP, 1999). Despite Roper Starch's ability to divide the very large cohort into five segments, the survey's overall statement is that it found "few differences among Baby Boomers of various demographic subgroups." There were few significant differences between females and males; likewise, there were few differences based on age or race/ethnicity. Similarly, various lifestage events play only a minor role in the outlook of Boomers. In relation to a limited number of retirement-related issues, divorce, job loss, or major illness seem to have affected the views of some Boomers. The major differences relate to income levels (AARP, 1999, p. 15). Health care expense was not considered a major concern by most in the survey; they seemed to feel that Medicare would still be available for their needs when they retired. Of course, the past eight years have seen an increase in prescription costs, health care costs have escalated faster than inflation in general, and there has been political discourse on several subjects relating to health care for the intervening years.

The Path Institute has developed a segmentation model for understanding, measuring, and predicting consumer health care attitudes and behavior. Its studies show that 90 percent of adults can be classified into one of nine groups with distinct and predictable patterns of health care use, trust in medical professionals, levels of compliance, and so forth (*Institute of Healthcare Improvement Newsletter,* 2002):

Clinic Cynic—Generally distrustful of the medical profession

Avoider—Refrains from using health care services until very sick or injured

Generic—Tends to balance a concern for cost with a concern for quality

Family Centered—Puts family health above everything else

Traditionalist—Willing to pay more for quality and tends to use the same providers

Loyalist—Characterized by moderation in health care opinions and behavior

Ready User—Actively seeks and uses health care services of all kinds

Independently Healthy—Very actively involved in his or her own health

Naturalist—Has a propensity to use nontraditional or alternative health care methods

This scheme seems to tie fairly well into the old VALS segmentation scheme, and, of course, parts of the Morgan and Levy (1993, 2002) segmentation schemes fit here also.

I have presented several different segmentation schemes that are based on health care concerns, more so than for any of the other items I have talked about, but there is a reason for this. Health care is a huge and growing industry; with the increasing age of the population it will continue to grow larger. We have gone from X-ray machines through computed tomography scans to magnetic resonance imaging—at a huge increase in cost, with a major increase in use needed to pay off the costs of the machines. We have drugs to control conditions that were hardly a problem a generation ago, and the drugs cost several hundred dollars a year. We are at a point where the human genome has been mapped, so we may be near the beginning of research that will eliminate many genetic disorders, and on and on. Yet there are still people who will only go to the doctor when they are seriously ill; the concept of preventive medicine is totally alien to them. Because we are now facing an "obesity epidemic" with its attendant disorders playing into an aging population for whom all of the conditions and disorders become more serious, we need to find ways to reach people and encourage them to take charge of their own health care and fit into Path Intstiute's "Independently Healthy" or Morgan and Levy's Proactives or whatever name this segment goes by in its particular scheme.

Before leaving the theme of health care segmentation, there is a need to discuss segmentation for special populations. There are several diseases and conditions that only affect specific genetically related populations. Sickle-cell anemia, which affects African Americans, and Tay-Sachs, which affects Ashkenazi Jews, are two examples. If one is dealing with sickle-cell anemia, there is no need to include the entire population because only African Americans develop the condition. A general segmentation scheme that then is cut to include only African Americans is what is needed. Because these conditions are not behavioral or lifestyle in origin, the type of segmentation scheme is less important than making sure that populations are excluded that do not suffer from the condition.

A different problem is HIV/AIDS. With the exception of those who have inherited one of the conditions from their infected mother or gotten it from a blood transfusion, they are primarily conditions of lifestyle. It is no longer merely considered a disease of the gay and drug users who use hypodermic needles, but these two groups of people represent by far the largest proportion of those affected in the United States. Despite many attempts to encourage the practice of safe sex and hypodermic syringe exchanges, HIV/AIDS continue to spread; there are reports that young gay males are again practicing sex without using condoms, apparently feeling either that the disease is under control or that the drug cocktails that research has yielded can slow the slide toward death. The problem with HIV/AIDS (in addition to the medical research into a cure) consists of changing people's risky behaviors into lower risk behaviors. There has been some research done into segmenting by behavior risk levels, particularly in trying to get people to cease smoking; however, there has not been much success reported.[2]

This chapter is about something more important than selling houses more quickly, or matching people with the right car, or manufacturing better-tasting food. It is about life and death. Unsafe sex, smoking, and eating too much and becoming obese or severely obese all shorten life expectancy and cause death and disease. If marketing can help reduce the unsafe behaviors then it will have risen above the "selling more soap" activity that it is often castigated as being. Trying to get people to the Ready User or Independently Healthy categories of the Path Institute's scheme, or whatever name by whatever firm these categories represent, is probably the highest social good that marketing or consumer research/science can perform for humanity. This would probably be a significant research project to perform alongside the NIH obesity research: how to sell the research so that people behave in a way that helps them.

REVIEW QUESTIONS

1. Does your family history have any of the markers for health risk commonly associated with aging? These include diabetes onset before age fifty, death by cardiovascular accident before age sixty-five, high serum cholesterol level, etc. If yes, are you doing anything to reduce your *personal* risk? If so, what? Why?
2. Do you follow the health-related news reports? Closely? Why?

SECTION V:
OTHER CONSIDERATIONS
AND DECISION-MAKING OVERLAYS

This section is the tool section. I explore the use of the Myers-Briggs Type Indicator as an overlay and an explanatory scheme for discussing lifestyle. I would strongly recommend that the reader go take the instrument. Most college counseling centers have access to it; it is available (in greater or lesser degree) online. Having come up with your Type, do some reading about Type and its meaning. It may be revelatory.

And then there is a case in how one firm explored in some depth and richness the meaning of applying a segmentation scheme to its understanding of its products . . .

Chapter 17

Myers-Briggs Type Indicator

Lifestyles, interests, values, expectations, and symbols by themselves do not explain the totality of our complex behaviors. We need to also consider *how* we think, not just *what* we think; we need to also consider *why* we behave in the ways we do, not just *how* we behave. Following the lead of Brooke Warrick, formerly of SRI, I have been using the Myers-Briggs Type Indicator (MBTI) for this purpose for a number of years. Warrick (1984) overlaid the MBTI onto the VALS typology with remarkable results.

The MBTI takes Carl Jung's psychology and examines how people differ along four simultaneous dimensions, creating sixteen Types (see Figure 17.1). The Type Instrument is fairly lengthy, although

SENSING		INTUITION			
THINKING	FEELING	FEELING	THINKING		
ISTJ	ISFJ	INFJ	INTJ	JUDGMENT	INTROVERSION
ISTP	ISFP	INFP	INTP	PERCEPTION	
ESTP	ESFP	ENFP	ENTP	PERCEPTION	EXTROVERSION
ESTJ	ESFJ	ENFJ	ENTJ	JUDGMENT	

FIGURE 17.1. Myers-Briggs—The sixteen types.

there are various Forms, some shorter, some longer. There is not a hint in either Jungian theory or the MBTI itself that one type is "better" than another; no therapist will try to "cure" you of your type. Furthermore, individuals' types do change, although the literature indicates that this is a rare occurrence. Also, one should always talk of "preferences"; although the other side of the dimension is still used, it is simply not preferred.

The first dimension is along Extraversion and Introversion. These words, as is true of the terms used in the rest of the MBTI analysis, as dimensions, do not mean precisely what they mean in English, but rather follow the psychology of Carl Jung as operationalized by Isabel Briggs Myers (Myers and Myers, 1980; Myers and McCaulley, 1985).

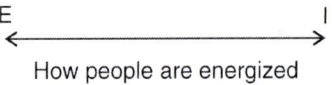

How people are energized

What energizes me most: interacting with people or being by myself? Which do I prefer *more:* to be around others or spend time by myself? Many projects or one at a time?

These questions are crucial for understanding people. Some of us are one, some the other. Neither is "right," nor is either "wrong." We just are. Personally, I am not energized by interacting with people; I do my best work closeted by myself. Working on one project through to completion is my preference, despite years of being a consultant for multiple clients—and only I can decide if that project is complete. I am a classic Introvert; I was once described as being so introverted as to be truly inside out—harsh, but not too far wrong.

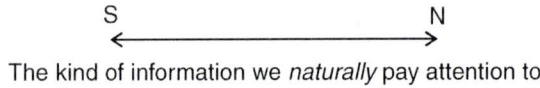

The kind of information we *naturally* pay attention to

Do I pay more attention to the facts and details, or do I try to understand the connections, underlying meaning, and implications? Am I down to earth and sensible or imaginative and creative? Which do I trust more: my direct experience or my gut? Am I in the here and now, or do I often imagine how things will affect the future?

Sensors are scientists; Intuitives are artists. This is clearly an over-simplification and is intended as such. Sensors are down to earth, not dreamers. They are the people who grab a wrench when they hear a noise under the hood, not the ones who stand there wondering what might be wrong. They are going to *find* out, not *figure* it out. They are the people of direct experience, the ones who trust only what their five senses tell them or have told them in the past.

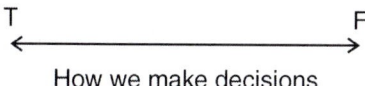
How we make decisions

Do I make decisions objectively, weighing the pros and cons or basing it on how I feel about the issue and how it will affect me personally? Am I logical and analytical or sensitive and empathetic? Is it more important to be truthful even if it hurts someone else's feelings or tactful even if it means telling a white lie? Which is more persuasive, a logical argument or an emotional appeal?

Whether a person is a Judger or a Perceptive is about how they make decisions. Are they logical, or do they work from a position of empathy? Do they always tell the truth, no matter where the chips may fall, or are they willing to shade the truth to avoid hurting someone's feelings? I have to emphasize again that neither of these stances, these preferences, is right or wrong. They just are. For Thinkers, this can be difficult to deal with.

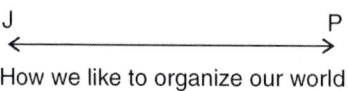
How we like to organize our world

Do I make decisions quickly and easily, or does making decisions make me anxious and unsure? Would I rather have things settled and decided or be able to leave my options open, just in case something comes up? Do I need to be in control, or can I let others call the shots? Am I conscious of time and always punctual, or am I always late and find that time has somehow slipped away? Am I very organized, or do I have trouble finding things? Work first or play first?

The Judgment-Perceptive dimension seems to me to be perhaps the most crucial of the four dimensions for many reasons. When you read the sentences discussing the opposition, it may strike you—as it did me—that this dimension can be a relationship killer, both of marriages and of friendships. I have a client who is an Extravert. He drove me nuts because he cannot think with his mouth closed; he has to talk his way through every problem. I have learned to just keep my figurative hearing aid turned off, grunt occasionally, but not listen to a word he says during this phase of things because nothing he says means anything, although I realize that this may sound pejorative.[1] However, the dimensions of decision making and time sense, of being organized (and what that concept actually means to the individuals) is so crucial to a relationship that if the people involved in that relationship do not understand each other's differences along that dimension, only problems will ensue, as anyone who uses the MBTI in marriage counseling will assert.

The MBTI has received a lot of support from two areas: educators and counselors, particularly those in relationship counseling. Educators adopted the MBTI particularly in response to their observing that different people learn differently—not so much at different speeds, but *differently*. Some people can read and understand what the author intended; some people have to manipulate physical objects to get the same understanding. Some people need to walk while they are thinking, some need music, some need total silence, and others need to go almost into a trance state to think. Counselors, particularly those involved with counseling relationships in trouble, also know that the different people in the relationship bring different temperaments, different understandings of so many of the concepts that make a relationship work that it is often very difficult for them to make changes, even if both of them are trying hard to make the relationship work through a difficult period, whether it is a specific difficulty with a marriage, or differences in parenting their children, or whatever the difficulty might be. Simply the difference between what the two individuals consider being "on time" can lead to constant arguing and an inability to do anything.

The Types are not randomly and uniformly distributed through the population. Hammer and Mitchell (1996) found that the national distribution of segments according to a survey based on the ethnic breakdown of the 1990 Census ran from 2.5 percent (ENFJ) to 15.6 percent (ISTJ) of the population (see Figure 17.2 for the entire distribution). Males and females have different distributions, although I do not in-

ISTJ	ISFJ	INFJ	INTJ
15.6 percent	11.5 percent	2.6 percent	3.5 percent
ISTP	ISFP	INFP	INTP
6.4 percent	4.5 percent	4.3 percent	5.2 percent
ESTP	ESFP	ENFP	ENTP
4.8 percent	5.7 percent	6.3 percent	4.7 percent
ESTJ	ESFJ	ENFJ	ENTJ
9.9 percent	9.6 percent	2.5 percent	2.8 percent

FIGURE 17.2. National type distribution of adults. *Source:* Hammer and Mitchell, 1996, p. 7.

tend to get deeply into the gender aspects (or the ethnic aspects) of the Type distributions; there is plenty of material available for those who wish to delve that deeply (particularly Hammer and Mitchell, 1996). The fact that the Types are not uniformly distributed may make it more difficult to communicate with the Types, but there are ways to cluster them that reduce the number of Types by reducing the dimensions on which they are divided. The method that probably has the most adherents and has had the most research done about it is the so-called Four Temperaments, discovered by David Kiersey (Kiersey, 1989; Kiersey and Bates, 1984). Kiersey states that those who are Sensing Judgmental (SJ), or Sensing Perceptive (SP), or Intuitive Feeling (NF), or Intuitive Thinking (NT) have more in common with each other than with those of the other Temperaments and that one can communicate with them accordingly. The Four Temperaments are not the only way to cut down the dimensions (see Cahill, 1996, pp. 87-91 for two other methods in use, particularly Figure 4.3 on p. 89).

Marketers can use the findings of the MBTI to ensure that their messages are heard and seen by those to whom they are aimed. Because the Types are so different from each other, crafting messages to specific types is not difficult; the difficulty is ensuring that the messages are seen only by those one wants to see them, that other Types do not see the messages and misunderstand them, causing problems in different segments.

An example of how to do this comes from my extensive research work with real estate agents. A few years ago I designed and fielded a major national survey for a client; we were interested in finding out major amounts of information from agents that had never been asked for other than perhaps by real estate firms about their own agents. The client authorized using the MBTI to see if we could actually find out what makes agents tick; he has been working with them as customers for over forty years and is often baffled by their reactions to his products and proposals. We received a large number of instruments back; when scored, I discovered that an extraordinary 75 percent of the agents were E—Js, populating only the bottom row of the Type table. Compare that with the Hammer and Mitchell (1996) national result shown in Figure 17.2 and you will see that real estate agents are three times as likely as the national population to be on that row. I searched journals and other reference materials to find another example of a sample that was so skewed to one row or column as this one but failed to find a single example.

In application, the findings of this survey are easy. We now know two major items about agents: they are MBTI Extraverts and thus are energized by being around people. This makes sense, because they are in personal-sales jobs. If they were not energized by people, they probably should leave the field. More unusual and important for dealing with them is the fact that they are Judgers—they are decisive, organized, punctual, and time-driven people. Anyone selling something to real estate agents should focus on these qualities in the words and images chosen for the marketing material. Probably more important is the fact that only those goods and services that appeal to these qualities in the agents will have much chance of success. This is part of the message of Warrick's (1984) work on overlaying the MBTI over VALS; VALS (or another psychographic segmentation scheme) may tell you who your market is, but it is not likely to tell you how to communicate well with them without some help (and the MBTI can certainly provide the assistance at very little additional direct cost for using the instrument) or to provide much in the way of additional training for management to be able to interpret the results of the instrument.

Continuing the example of real estate agents, Extroverts are likely to do the following (Lawrence, 1982, pp. 69-77):

Choose to work with a group
Plunge into new experiences
Be relaxed and self-confident
Be interested in others and their doings
Readily offer opinions
Share personal experiences
Want to experience things so that they understand them
Ask questions to check on the expectations of the group or leader
Dislike complicated procedures and get impatient with slow jobs
Eagerly attend to interruptions
Act quickly, often without thinking
Like to work by trial and error

Judgers are likely to do the following (Lawrence, 1982, pp. 69-77):

Like to have things decided and settled
Be more decisive than curious
Live according to plans
Live according to standards and customs not easily or lightly set aside
Try to make situations conform to their standards
Make definite choices from among possibilities
Be uneasy with unplanned happenings
Like to have assignments be clear and definite
Be tolerant of routine procedures

Thus, one can begin to see a pattern of communications that a manager could use with his or her employees who are E—Js; it also shows what a company that is trying to sell to real estate agents should emphasize in its marketing. This is what Myers-Briggs can offer without years and years of experience and training.

REVIEW QUESTIONS

If your college counseling service offers the service, take the extended Myers-Briggs Type Indicator and discuss the results with one of the professionals. Otherwise, log on to the Internet at one of the many sites that offer some version of the Indicator for free and take it.

1. What is your Type? Based on your discussion with the counselor and your reading, do you feel this accurately describes you?
2. What is the distribution of Types in the class?
3. Do you think your class represents the Type distribution of the United States? Why?

Chapter 18

Family Considerations

Segmentation is an individual fact. However, many products are bought by couples and/or families, and families then should be the unit of segmentation. Nevertheless, there has been little research into family purchase decision making or even husband-wife (or other dyadic) behavior. Industrial marketing has dealt with buying committees for years, but in consumer research the heavy preponderance of research has been on individuals. For most segmentation schemes, this is not an issue, but PRIZM works on the basis of Zip Codes, and there is usually more than one person in a residence—are they all the same PRIZM type? What about VALS?

Arnold Mitchell did some work on couples under the VALS typology (Mitchell, 1984); the study broke new ground for SRI because it was the first time that it had studied interactions among different VALS types. There are a number of implications drawn. First, over half of those who are married are married to spouses of the same VALS type; however, this means that not quite half came from forty-four different combinations, of which only one comprised more than 5 percent of marriages. Second, Achievers were members of 44 percent of all marriages—double their representation in the population; furthermore, Achievers powerfully influence family purchase decisions. Third, in marriage in which two VALS types are present, the "dominant" partner seems to be the partner at the "higher" level in the VALS typology. If VALS is gone, why bring up this work? Simply, I have seen nothing like it elsewhere, certainly not in a publicly available segmentation scheme, and the implications of this work are powerful.

The fact that half of the married couples are a single VALS type makes it possible to treat married couples as a single unit for marketing purposes, making communicating much easier. This feeds into the Myers-Briggs Type Indicator (MBTI) work on couples, which indicates that there are often significant differences in MBTI types in a marriage. This would indicate that perhaps most of the MBTI work that indicates that there are differences in type are dealing with the half of the married couples who have different VALS types.

Furthermore, the fact that Achievers were represented in 44 percent of the marriages is not surprising when one knows VALS and the Achiever type. These are people for whom convention is important, for whom doing the expected thing is crucial. Living together as unmarried couples or being single (certainly in 1984 when Mitchell's work was done) was not something that people who were rather conventional and who wanted to succeed in business or many of the professions did in large numbers. Furthermore, Achievers are by their nature quite dominant in most settings; the Societally Conscious tend not to be dominated by Achievers but would rather withdraw from the situation. Other types tend to be dominated, so the fact that Achievers have the strongest voice in their family purchase decisions is not surprising.

These findings are important even though VALS is gone. We have not been able to perform similar research on the Tribes; I would expect that many of these findings would hold true for the Tribes, however. Can we lean on the VALS findings insofar as the Tribes are concerned? No, but the findings are suggestive of approaches that need to be taken when marketing to couples, other dyads, and families with goods and services in which those are the normal buying decision makers. Designing marketing programs for new cars is a clear example that may well include a dyadic decision, and knowing how to approach the dyad is important. Is one member of the dyad the decision maker for making financial decisions and the other for picking the product? Real estate agents have long claimed that it is easy for them to get women involved in the search process for a house; it is the men who are difficult to reach. Can real estate firms start working toward a way to reach the dyad as a dyad instead? Can they figure out a way to reach men, particularly if they know enough about the female half of the dyad? Because this is now 2006, what about unmarried couples, both heterosexual and gay? What are their dyadic buying patterns? Are they same as married couples', or different?

Working with dyads is not easy; anyone who works with married couples, whether they are counseling troubled marriages or working with couples trying to get married, will attest to this fact. There often is a dominant partner; does one address that partner's needs, or does one try to work with the couple as a couple? There is a different approach needed for each, and ignoring the needs of the couple as couple can be quite harmful over time, but "the squeaky wheel gets the grease" in counseling as in most other venues in life. Segmenting couples is not easy, either.

The role of the family in lifestyle segmentation is problematic. The family needs to be examined both as a segmentation unit and as a target market. Much has been written in the past decade or so about the family and the changes it has undergone since World War II, as well as further changes it will undoubtedly undergo in the future. However, little of this material has addressed the role of the family as a buying unit.

Directing attention to the family as a buying unit is an obvious action to take given the product categories that I have examined, because cars, houses, food, and health care are all purchased and consumed in the context of families and family life. Houses are built primarily for families; most automobile ads are aimed at heads of families. Life insurance is aimed directly at people to provide income for their family after they have died. However, this is the twenty-first century, and the composition of the family has changed since the end of World War II and continues to change. The "traditional" family—which turns out to be typical and traditional in the United States only of the families in which the Baby Boom generation was raised—of father at work, mother at home, two-point-something children all living by themselves in a house surrounded by grass—is no longer the dominant means of organizing a family, and marketers need to recognize this fact because it has tremendous implications for how goods and services will be delivered, bought, packaged, and consumed in the future.

For example, what does "family size" mean today? Big enough for a family of four? What about a family in which the parents are divorced but share custody of the children 50-50? What about when the older of the two-point-something children goes off to college? What about if the parents remarry? Or if the couple is gay and has no children? Or does? Detergent packages need to be rethought, obviously, but what about houses? If both parents of a divorced family share custody, how much room do the children need? In each house? What about if the parents remarry, and their spouses also share custody? These are not idle questions; the bewildering possibilities of family size and composition make it difficult to deal with the family as a target unit or a decision-making unit in marketing decisions, but nothing in the family seems to have changed to indicate that the family is no longer the appropriate unit for housing or food or life insurance.

The necessity to have marketers consider the family is the fact that only in this way can marketers confront the decision-making unit. If the head of household is truly the target for a product such as life insurance, do not focus on the family. If the family is the unit that is truly making the decisions, such as about houses, some of the cars, furniture, college educations, etc., then focus on the family as the decision-making unit for the marketing efforts. Again, I will stress that it is important to separate the decision maker from the buyer from the user of the product or service; in fact, it is probably more important than ever to do so because more families fragment and re-form—one can never be sure who is actually going to the store to buy the product or going online to order it.

Dealing with the family as a family adds two other levels of complexity to the segmentation scheme and marketing effort. Family decisions usually take more time to make than decisions by individuals. More people's opinions need to be heard, and more people's needs and wants must be considered. In this sense, family marketing looks somewhat like organizational marketing, with its long lead times, buying committees, and increased formal consideration of information before the decision can be made. The second complexity is learning how to communicate with each member of the family as well as the family as a unit. If dealing with a dyad is difficult for marketers (or psychologists), how much more difficult must it be to deal with a family, particularly when there is no single definition of what a family is, particularly as that family's composition changes over time.

Life-stage segmentation, also called the "family life cycle," is the recognition that a family's needs and expenditures (and composition) change over time as people leave their parents' home(s), marry, have children, and grow up to repeat the cycle. In a sense, life-stage segmentation represents family-based demographics, particularly age and income level. The focus on longitudinal changes in purchases is valuable for predicting macroeconomic demand for specific products such as houses, refrigerators, nursery sets, retirement planning, nursing-home demand, etc., although it can also be useful for demand for specific brands. The advertising campaign of several years ago that had the tag line "This is not your father's Oldsmobile" typified the longitudinal, generational approach.

Life-stage analysis has traditionally included the following eight categories:

1. *Young Single Stage*—Young is relative, but the title is now usually used to mean those who have never been married. This group has a lower income than some of the others but also has smaller financial responsibilities. This is the group frequently targeted for entertainment—ski packages and similar products and services.
2. *Newly Married Stage*—Still young (and childless). This is a relatively small (but seemingly growing) group with substantial buying activity. This is the stage when houses and furnishings, white goods (stoves, refrigerators, etc.), dishes, and other consumer durables tend to be bought in a relatively short time span.
3. *Full Nest I Stage*—Children have appeared, with the youngest not yet in school. Financial squeezing now truly appears; discretionary spending may be at its lowest point, particularly if one parent has not yet returned to the workforce or is only working part time.
4. *Full Nest II Stage*—Youngest child is now in school. Both parents are now probably working (if this is intended), so the squeeze is somewhat reduced. Discretionary spending is still low, but purchases of children's goods and services are high.
5. *Full Nest III Stage*—The children are now teenagers. Expenditure patterns now represent the replacement of durables bought during the Newly Married Stage that have worn out or have become otherwise undesirable as well as the purchase of additional durables. Furthermore, vacations and travel become more prevalent than during the previous two stages.
6. *Empty Nest I Stage*—The children have left home and entered their own Young Single Stage. The financial squeeze on the parents is over, leaving them free to travel, pursue hobbies, and substantially improve the house.

7. *Empty Nest II Stage*—The couple has retired, and income has consequently declined. However, given the drastic reduction in necessary expenditures, discretionary expenditures may well be substantially increased. They may move to a smaller house or apartment, reducing the need to replace durables one more time; the second car may be given up. However, spending on grandchildren may be quite high.

8. *Solitary Survivor Stage*—One partner is now widowed. Income again is low, as is financial responsibility, but medical expenses may absorb all of the previously discretionary income.

The explanatory power of the family life-cycle concept is clear; it defines the trajectory of a family over time in terms of financial responsibilities and purchases as the demographic make up of the family changes. One may quibble that three "Full Nest Stages" are not necessary or that not everyone goes through every stage; however, a more damning weakness is obvious: this cycle above describes the "traditional" family of *Leave It to Beaver* or Ozzie and Harriet Nelson. This is not the trajectory of the families of the twenty-first century.

The family of the twenty-first century is, of course, nothing if not diverse, and the diversity truly took off in the 1990s. College-graduate children move back home, disrupting what would have been an Empty Nest. Composite families might have been Full Nest III, but after remarriage by the partners now technically they become Full Nest I because one of the (step)children is still not in school or the partners have children of their own (Johnson and Roberts, 1992). Divorce creates two families—one of which has no full-time children and only one adult, the other having the full-time children. Alternatively, divorce creates two families with half-time children in the place of one family with full-time children. Some 35 percent of Americans are now "intertwined in stepfamilies" (Zaslow, 2004). What do we call it when two people with adult children get married? And so on and so forth. These changes in family composition need to be recognized in any segmentation scheme that purports to deal with family life cycles. Swallow (2004) chronicles her journey through exactly these changes as she divorced, stayed single for a while, sharing custody of her two children with her ex-husband, and subsequently remarried, continuing to share custody of her children and her new husband's children (with his ex-wife) in a bewildering whirlpool of "who is in the house today?" and groping toward a definition of "what is a family?"

Despite the great descriptive power of the concept of the family life cycle, communication with people in the various stages is difficult, because the stage may not coincide well with any demographic variable. Not only are many in the Young Single Stage older than Empty Nesters of any stage—and thus subject to being offended by the medium used to communicate with others in that stage—many in the Solitary Survivor Stage are younger than those in Empty Nest II, with the same possibility. As Tinney (1989) points out tongue in cheek, "Life Begins When the Kids Leave Home and the Dog Dies—But That's Where the Family Life Cycle Ends." She reminds us that not everyone over the median age is the same, that not all Baby Boomers or Generation Xs are alike. Furthermore, our children continue to influence our spending even after they are not part of the household but remain part of the family. Nevertheless, marketers have kept trying to fine-tune the concept (Lofland and Razzouk, 1992; Scaninger and Danko, 1993). Roberts et al. (1992) redefine the family life-cycle concept a bit in a valiant and possibly fruitful attempt to separate "families" from "households." They do this by including the ages of the individuals in the household, the number of people present, the kinship situation(s) and psychic involvement(s) of the members, and the financial resource variables and the allocation involvement(s).

Furthermore, other variables may be as predictive and descriptive. Goodwin and Lockshin (1992) suggest that marketers need to learn to adapt to consumers who present themselves alone to shop, to eat in restaurants, and to travel. Marketers have failed to do so very well to date. Are solo consumers lonely, or are they simply alone? As the family changes composition, with several stages during which someone may be a solo "family"—from a young unmarried to a recently divorced or widowed individual to an elderly survivor—these solo consumers will have different wants and needs that marketers must be aware of. However, communicating with solo consumers will always be difficult. I believe that the family life cycle is one of those tools that is descriptive rather than prescriptive.

In a children's book titled *Love You Forever* (Munsch and McGraw, 1997) a boy is cared for tenderly by his mother; as he grows up, they have a parent and adult child relationship, which shifts as the mother grows very old and frail and the adult child cares for the frail old parent. Encapsulated in a quite sentimental book is the story of so many of us; with both divorce rates and the actuarial table at work, we are cared for by our mothers but have to care for them when they become old because our fathers (and, in many cases, their subsequent husbands) predecease them or are otherwise absent. At both ends of this cycle, someone is making decisions for another person that marketers need to know about and to understand the dynamics and mechanisms by which those decisions are made and implemented.

An example of this dilemma for marketers is who *chooses* the family's food as opposed to who *buys* it. This is not the example that was prevalent in the early 1970s (and probably earlier) when I was working on my MBA: what happens to the wife who brings home a six-pack of beer that isn't the brand her husband wants?[1] The question of who chooses the food has become of paramount importance during the epidemic of obesity mentioned in Chapter 16; lifetime obesity is now showing up in relatively young children in large numbers, and nutritionists and psychologists are placing the ultimate blame for this fact on parents. "I don't know of any little child who jumps in the car and drives to a supermarket and buys their own food," said Dan Jaffe, executive vice president for government relations at the Association of National Advertisers, an organization based in Washington whose members include food companies (Buss, 2004). Of course, as was mentioned during the earlier discussion of the Tween market, there is the "whine" factor at the grocery store or when choosing which restaurant to go to; parents often simply give in to their children because of fatigue or desire not to be seen as an ogre or for any one of a number of reasons. However, the issue here is "who is actually choosing the food?" or restaurant or beer. If marketers assume that the buyer is the one who chooses, then one strategy is necessary; if they assume that the user is the one who chooses and the buyer is simply the payer in the transaction, then another strategy is necessary. If there is a mutual choice, then yet a third strategy has to be implemented.

When we discuss children's products or food aimed at children, this marketing truth is relatively evident. Children rarely buy their own items without parental involvement, at least until they hit the Tween years and possibly even later. However, when we discuss the reversed role of a child caring for an older parent, this truth is somewhat hidden. It is hidden because we expect adults to be able to express preferences on goods and services and act on those preferences. However, as so many of the old find out, aging past a certain point involves losing control over one's choices and, in many respects, over one's life itself.

Therefore, how do we market the products and services for the old? Do we segment on the users' psychographics or the buyers'? Who is the decision maker in the dyad? One would hope that after a lifetime relationship with our parents we would know what they want even if they cannot articulate their wishes themselves, but we know this is not always the case—and sometimes, even if we do know, we cannot provide that choice.

I speak from personal experience in this matter. My parents retired to an RV full time for three years, followed by a decision to settle in Eugene, Oregon, where they lived for seventeen years before my father died. My mother expressed a wish to stay in their house, which we were able to do for the next four years, despite the ravages of increasing stroke-caused dementia, with a bit of juggling of caregivers, sometimes part time and sometimes full time. However, recently we have had to face the demands of increasing care and decreasing finances; my mother went into an adult foster home in August 2004—not against her will but not by choice. The choice of which foster home was neither hers nor mine; it was decided by the fact that only one home in the area would allow her to retain her cat, sent to her by a nephew to take care of. She no longer has many choices: her meals are planned by the caregivers, her schedule is likewise—she is allowed to choose her clothing. We are at the end of the *Love You Forever* story. The decision maker for the four residents of the foster home is now operating, in the old categories of marketing, as an industrial-marketing buyer.

REVIEW QUESTIONS

1. Do you think your parents fit into the same Tribe/VALS type that you do? Why?
2. Does your spouse/significant other (if you have one) fit within your same Tribe/VALS type? Why?
3. At what point along the "traditional" family life-cycle stage are you? List purchases made in the past year that seem to fit that stage. List purchases that do not seem to fit.

Chapter 19

Case and Thoughts

CASE

In 1988, the client of mine who was a VALS subscriber decided to find out if the different VALS groups wanted different things in real estate classified advertising. Could segmentation be used to write different newspaper advertisements to make houses appeal to different segments of customers? Could it be used to make the same house appeal to more than one segment of customer rather than use the traditional feature-driven advertisement that seeks to appeal to everyone by focusing on no one and forcing the focus onto the product? Something needs to be done because the state of classified real estate advertising is bad; in 1997, *The Wall Street Journal* reviewed its home-of-the-week feature, which specialized in houses then going for more than $1 million; only fourteen of eighty-one listings had sold, with four more under contract (Paik, 1997). Although there are many reasons why houses do not sell, advertising that does not appeal to those who are more apt than others to buy is also a suspected culprit.

National Market Measures (NMM), a Cleveland, Ohio, research firm, was commissioned to hold three focus groups: one each for Belongers, Achievers, and the Societally Conscious. These three VALS types were hypothesized to have the greatest importance for real estate publishing because of the size of the groups and their income and wealth levels. Nationally, Belongers constituted 38 percent of the population, Achievers 20 percent, and the Societally Conscious 12 percent (Ploss, 1987); in the Cleveland area Belongers were 35 percent, Achievers 31 percent, and the Societally Conscious 12 percent (WJW-TV8, 1988). Thus, with three focus groups, the client would have data from the three VALS types that represented over two-thirds of the adult population and a considerably larger percentage of the house-buying population. It was hoped that the information that came out of the research would be useable in the geographically dispersed markets served by the client (Lesser and Hughes, 1986).

NMM used telephone solicitation with a screening questionnaire that disguised the subject to be covered but did ascertain that the respondent was either "actively in the market to buy a house or had recently bought or sold a house." The respondents who agreed to participate were sent the VALS questionnaire and were VALS typed by SRI; only those who were Belongers, Achievers, or Societally Conscious were to be recontacted and scheduled for a group. One problem surfaced during the typing; there were not enough Societally Conscious individuals who were "actively" in the market to form a group; the decision was made to include enough Experientials (5 percent of the national population and 6.5 percent in Cleveland) to have a full group of what SRI called Inner Directeds—a larger grouping of types. Experientials and Societally Conscious had profiles more similar to each other than either was to Belongers or Achievers.

Each focus group was shown color photographs of ten different houses; the photographs were mounted on flip charts in chronological order of the house style. These houses were all actually for sale, although not in Cleveland; they were deliberately chosen to represent house styles that are commonly found around Cleveland to make the participants more comfortable dealing with them. Although they were cut out of several different for-sale magazines and represented several different real estate markets, they were all listed in the $300,000 to $500,000 range; the participants were told that the price of the house would not matter, that they were to assume that they could afford any of the houses that they would be shown. At this point there were really only three questions that the client wanted answered by the participants:

1. Which house style(s) did each VALS type prefer and why?
2. What further information would each VALS type wish to see in an advertisement for that house?
3. What language did each VALS type use to talk about the houses?

The Achiever group that was held in May was problematic; the moderator stated—and later the people at SRI who listened to the tape of the group agreed—that she had never had to work so hard to get a group to respond. It was almost impossible to get one member of the group to respond in an undirected manner to a comment of another group member. The recommendation of both the moderator and SRI was to hold another focus group of Achievers. Thus there were ultimately four groups: Belongers with six participants, Inner Directeds with nine, and two Achiever groups with nine in one and ten in the other.

With regard to Question 1—did the groups respond differently to the different house styles presented to them—the answer is clearly "Yes." Table 19.1 presents the top three choices of the VALS types. Although there is some overlap among the groups—Tudor Revival was picked by both the Inner Directeds and Achievers, and Modern and Norman/French Revival were picked by both Achievers and Belongers—the rank order was different except for Modern. More important, perhaps, is the fact that the reasons given by participants for their choices were quite different. These reasons are discussed below.

With regard to Question 2—what information was needed beyond the photograph—there were similarities among the VALS types as well as striking differences. All participants stressed the need for location (the actual street address by preference), price, size of the house and/or lot—the "usual" information contained in most real

TABLE 19.1. Preferred house styles by VALS Type.

VALS type	House styles
Inner Directed	1. Turn of the Century
	2. Tudor Revival
	3. Georgian/Colonial Revival
Achievers	1. Modern
	2. Norman/French Revival
	3. Tudor Revival
Belongers	1. Modern
	2. Ranch
	3. Norman/French Revival

Source: National Market Measures, 1998, pp. 17-25.

estate classified advertisements. The Inner Directeds wanted some indication of the interesting features and overall *gestalt* of the house. They were willing to overlook the absence of a list of features in return for more psychological attributes, mostly in the nature of making the house more "interesting"—a key word for this group. The Achievers wanted to know about utilities, how long the house had been on the market, and the age of the house. Their biggest need, however, was that the house appear to be a trophy, a visible sign of the fact that they have "made it." The Belongers had a very narrow list of information requirements: size of the kitchen, size and number of closets and bedrooms, as well as what school district the house was in. Overall, however, the Belongers seemed to express the need for location as the primary criterion for their choice. All of the information desired by all groups can, of course, be obtained by a tour of the house and grounds; these data are what these VALS types want in order to make the decision to make the tour and are thus crucial to include in advertisements designed to make them want to come to look.

In other words, segmentation of communications content is important; if one wants Belongers to view a house, an advertisement containing Achiever content would not work. Although this is "obvious," all too often managers seem to think that if the product attributes are different for different segments' products, a firm has finished its segmentation work. However, these focus groups proved yet again that it is at least as important to segment the message content as it is to segment the attributes of the product itself.

Question 3—the different word choices and symbols to use in classified advertisements for the different VALS types—remained unanswered by this research. So much time was spent in determining favored house styles and lists of features that the groups spent insufficient time developing word lists. One would like to work with the word lists in conjunction with McCracken's concept of a Diderot Unity—"highly consistent complements of consumer goods" (McCracken, 1988, p. 120)—to see if his concept holds for talking about goods as well as the goods themselves; my supposition is that it does hold. The groups provided insufficient data to put forward a formal proposition, but there are indications here of what might be apparent "hot buttons" to reach different VALS types in advertisements, as well as the equally important words *not* to use.

There were really two different sets of implications of this research: those for my client and others in their real estate publications, and wider implications for real estate brokerage firms and real estate development firms. To take the second implication first, it is clear that the different VALS types view house styles differently. Although only the Inner Directed group seemed comfortable putting "correct" names on the different house styles,[1] different styles clearly appealed to different groups and, at least as important, three styles—contemporary, NeoVictorian, and colonial—were no one's favorite, and few participants could find a kind word to say about any of these three. It would be beneficial for a developer to be careful when choosing which house styles to build in a development, unless it was the developer's conscious choice to try to mix the three VALS types studied here in the same development.

It was the answer to Question 2—what information beyond the picture would be needed by each VALS type—that holds the greatest interest. One of the participants stated that he needed "nothing—the picture says it all." Although this statement is a more extreme statement of the Achiever position than the other participants were willing to make, it was basically confirmed by the other Achievers in that group. The sentiment was also confirmed by the auditors at SRI when they reviewed the tape as being quite consistent with one of the differences between Achievers and the Inner Directeds: Inner Directeds like to read lots of copy in an advertisement, whereas Achievers will hardly read copy.

It should then be theoretically possible to design a single publication to reach both Achievers and the Inner Directeds with advertisements that only the targeted group would "see" even though there were two ads for a single house. The ad for the Inner Directeds would have a small picture and lots of copy; the Achiever ad would have an enormous picture and a headline containing only the information mentioned earlier as vital to Achievers. In fact, after listening to the groups, it became apparent that the Inner Directeds had the uncanny ability to look "through" the pictures presented to them (all of which were simply standard real estate front elevation pictures) and state categorically what the inside of the house looked like, how it was laid out, down to floor plans and window locations on the sides of the house away from the camera. It might be possible to target ads at the

Inner Directeds by giving them only an interior shot and the house style in the body copy.

It is clear, even from the exceedingly preliminary nature of this set of focus groups, that there are differences in how houses are perceived by different people—even when the houses are viewed only in 3×5 color photographs. Using a psychographic typology such as VALS to segment respondents sharpens differences among houses. Jack L. Nasar used an intercept study in which his researchers showed people stylized drawings of six house types to determine which house people would feel most comfortable about approaching if they needed help, which house would have someone who was a "take-charge" individual live, and which house would people choose if they won a "dream-house" lottery. Nasar found that there were clear differences among house types along these dimensions, although there is no indication that he tried to differentiate between types of people in his intercept sample (Freudenheim, 1988; Nasar, 1988a, 1989). Sadalla et al. (1987) performed different research with similar results—that our houses reflect who we are. Shortly after his research was published, Nasar started using images of real buildings captured on a graphic computer system "manipulated for appropriate control," because he felt that the drawings he had been using might produce ambiguous results (Nasar, 1988b). The need to control landscape features in this fashion was pointed up by all three VALS types commenting on the contemporary house's lack of established trees being a negative having nothing to do with the style of the house, but in The Forest City of Cleveland, no large trees in a neighborhood is a definite negative.

It is evident that, unless house styles are intermingled in a neighborhood, the likelihood of different VALS types of the same income level living together in that neighborhood is lessened. The Inner Directeds would not be comfortable in Achiever houses and vice versa.[2] This finding has great potential meaning in at least two respects. First is that mixing house styles is uncommon in new housing developments; therefore, the likelihood of different VALS types living together is at least hypothetically higher in older, more "organic" communities, which may at least in part explain the attraction these communities have for the Inner Directeds. Second is that it is at least theoretically possible for lifestyle or psychographic data to be used by others than marketers—planners, for example—in an attempt to plan the future growth and trends for their cities. However, it is also clear from this project that there are distinct and meaningful differences among individuals in the real estate market that the VALS typology is identifying. The responses of the Inner-Directed participants resembled each other far more than they did the responses of the Achiever participants and vice versa. I am not claiming superiority for VALS here over the Tribes or any other psychographic segmentation scheme; my point is simply that there is "something" out there that VALS captured. These differences among the types are real and systematic, and they produce actionable results. Thus, the real estate industry's focus on property location as the most important feature of a house may have members of that industry aimed in an inappropriate direction for talking to their prospective customers.

Csikszentmihalyi and Rochberg-Halton (1981) discuss the three ways in which their respondents described their houses: the architectural style, the number and functions of the rooms, and the peculiarities that make the dwelling unique to the respondent. This mixture of descriptions suggested to these authors that Americans were relying on previous forms of aesthetic order for coherence, that there is a lack of a cultural goal that imposes itself on the shape of our houses. Alternatively, this variety can be seen as a sign of individuality. Our houses are such a major defining portion of who we are in society that we look for that which differentiates us from our neighbors, not what ties us together with them. However, to continue with using VALS, Belongers do *not* wish to differentiate themselves from their neighbors, at least not insofar as the *outside* of their house is concerned (and probably not insofar as the inside is concerned, either, but the research did not address the question) the Inner Directeds, however, *do* want to differentiate their houses from those of their neighbors, both inside and out.

However, VALS clearly cannot stand alone in the segmentation effort, at least in discussions of the advertising for housing. There are at least two reasons for this. First, purchasing a house is frequently not an individual decision; often there are spouses and/or significant other(s) to be included in the decision of which house to buy (Munsinger et al., 1975). Although the research discussed here did not approach this point directly, it is obvious that—because VALS along with all the other segmentation schemes I have ever seen only type individuals and not families—this fact may be a problem. It would be less of a problem for a communications program than, say, building houses for resale if there were patterns in which type marries which type (and VALS did some interesting preliminary work along these lines [Mitchell, 1984]). For a communications program one might have to spend more to ensure that both halves of a dyad, for example, saw an advertisement. Second, there are at least life-cycle considerations that may supersede psychographic type on occasion. One of the participants in the Inner-Directed group kept commenting about wanting more closets, rooms with doors rather than an open plan, and other similar items when discussing interiors. One of the people behind the glass kept complaining that the participant must really be a Belonger who should not have been in the group. Her Inner-Directed score was not high, but not borderline Belonger, either. It later developed that she had three children under the age of five and simply wanted places to be able to put things away and to be able to get away from her children. No usable, practical psychographic segmentation model would surface that fact, yet this fact would be crucial in this person's choice of a house—at least at the time of the focus groups.

Furthermore, even VALS types are not homogeneous. No group that represents 38 percent of the population, as does Belongers, or even 20 percent of the population, as does Achievers, can be homogeneous. That the client had to hold two Achiever groups because of differences in the groups' abilities to verbalize points this fact out. Different marketing programs would clearly be needed to deal with the two different sets of Achievers that the client needed; the MBTI overlay might work here. Nevertheless, it is apparent that the internal differences within the types are far outweighed by the external differences between types. This is, of course, the basis for segmentation as a means of directing marketing efforts to a target market.

THOUGHT ONE

One of the issues surrounding segmentation is the degree to which the seller discloses the segmentation to the buyers. Given the cute names often used for the segments and the fact that many of those in the marketing and advertising communities make the descriptions of many of the segments sound quite derogatory, it is often probably not a good idea for buyers to know about the segmentation scheme (or, in fact, the fact of segmentation at all). There is almost nothing in generally available material to indicate how buyers would react. However, one tantalizing finding arose from a research opportunity in 1994 (see Cahill and Polansky, 1997, for the details). Prior to doing the research, Sharon Polanksy (of Gallup Applied Science) and I had hypothesized that people would be interested in the segmentation typology but that they would be offended by the use of the typology in an applied marketing case—a real estate agent's eyeing them, trying to figure out which type they were in order to sell them a specific house. We were surprised, therefore, when 10 percent said that they would find the segmentation very useful and 50 percent somewhat useful. This implies that some buyers are willing to be typecast in a segment if they believe that the typecasting will expedite the buying process.

In 2003, Douthit Communications, Inc. (DCI), was exploring the possibility of producing and delivering its *Homes Illustrated* magazines over the Internet. As part of that exploration, the firm had designed a site on the World Wide Web for listings of houses for sale with descriptions and photographs and wished to expose the design to consumers. Two focus groups were held in Cleveland, Ohio, in October. The screening criteria were people between ages thirty and fifty-five years with household incomes in excess of $40,000 who had purchased a house in the past two years or were expecting to purchase a house within the next year. The groups were separated into a group of males and a group of females; the researchers' experience has been that if the group is to explore technological issues, gender separation extracts better answers from women. The researchers were also going to take advantage of this opportunity to determine whether the different Tribes viewed the house-search process differently.

Since the original study using the Tribes reported in Cahill and Polansky (1997), the Tribes had evolved from six into five. Also in the mix now was the fact that a scoreable instrument had been developed so that individuals could be placed into a Tribe with some degree of confidence that they had been placed into the correct Tribe. The members of the focus groups were mailed the instrument when they agreed to come to the group; the instruments were all sent in for scoring prior to the groups meeting.

Early in the two-hour focus-group experiences, the group members had their instruments returned with the proper Tribe written on it. Only the individual knew what Tribe he or she belonged in; this information was not made public. Both groups initially favored having the Tribes information—taken as a generic concept—as part of the house-buying process. The participants were interested in the possibilities and capabilities of being matched to houses by their lifestyles; females seemed more interested in it than the males. The women agreed that they would prefer a search process that would narrow down a field of choices; the men preferred being able to observe all potential real estate properties on the market.

Then the moderator provided the individuals with the descriptions given in Exhibit 19.1. In addition to the written descriptions, each of the Tribes now has a pictorial representation of the people and activities "typical" of the Tribe, which the group members also saw. As the individuals started reading the descriptions, they became uncomfortable. Then the negative comments began. The women's group stated categorically that the Tribes reminded them of horoscopes, becasue they felt as if someone else was informing them of the nature of their personality. The men's group did not focus on horoscopes, but their comments were also clearly negative. The moderator quickly had to change to the next item in the discussion guide to avoid having the whole research effort collapse in the face of the resentment of the groups to the Tribe descriptions.

What caused the different reactions between the exit interviews in 1994 and the focus groups in 2003? There seems to be three reasons, all of which may have an impact on segmentation strategies.

First, in 1994, the respondents self-selected their own Tribe from a brief description, whereas in the 2003 focus groups an instrument was used to place people into a Tribe. There was a lot of comment in both focus groups that "I see parts of me in two of the Tribes"—a not uncommon issue in any typology.

Second, the descriptions in the 1994 version (Exhibit 19.2) were essentially nonpejorative and quite benign. By 2003 the descriptions had become much less benign. The women's group objected to the word "macho" in the definition of Upkeepers; a couple of the men objected to the "interest in motor sports" in the same definition. There seems to be a tendency in describing typology groups to write "down" for some of the groups. Typologies are designed by professionals— either academics or marketing researchers—and these types of people tend to be in the segments near the "top" of typologies; the descriptions of both Achievers and Authenticks in Exhibit 19.1 are

EXHIBIT 19.1.
People Descriptions of the Tribes Scheme in 2003

Authenticks

Creative people of achievement and success with personal or unusual home choices. Life, to you, is a path to explore, not a goal to achieve. You care more about being unique than owning what is unique. You are likely to be highly educated, professional, anti-status. You value privacy, being close to nature. You probably prefer pre-owned houses best. You then "make" the house to reflect your inner-directed values and lifestyles.

Trenders

You are younger, upward striving and want the Achiever lifestyle. You're hardworking, with both husband and wife holding down full-time jobs. But for now you'll settle for statusy touches. Your ideal home would be loaded with features, even if it's small. You're often on a tight budget and must settle for below-average priced homes; perhaps a nest, hidden away from the world, or, a front elevation that makes a big statement to the street.

Achievers

True pace-setters in business or professional fields, you expect homes that will reflect status. High-income, education, occupation, you prefer eye-catching homes with all the status features. You are "outer directed," taking cues from those you admire. Your lifestyle focuses attention on self, work, family. You want a home to reflect yourself; stylish and good-looking. And, being far-seeing, your home should be marketable.

Heartlanders

You are a traditionalist in lifestyle, interests, and values. You want your path through life to be narrow, well-lit, well-posted. Security is very important. You want a solid, nonshowy home in a neighborhood peopled by people like you. Nostalgia and family are big with you. You are great joiners and excellent club members. And you want your "next" home to be the last.

Upkeepers

You keep America running as mechanics, carpenters, growers, machine-tool makers. You're patriotic, macho, like sports, especially those to do with motors, and like to fish and hunt. You are very individualistic and self-sufficient, being the quintessential "do it yourselfers." Your ideal home is on the outskirts with at least an acre, allowing space for rec vehicles, places to work on cars, and a vegetable garden.

EXHIBIT 19.2.
People Descriptions of the Tribes Scheme in 1994

Winners

Highest income, education, occupation; lots of status display—want the Monument House. Winners want the biggest, most expensive of everything.

Trenders

Young, upward strivers, they have champagne tastes but beer budgets. They want everything the Winners have.

Upkeepers

Blue collar, low education. They are just getting by. They want the basics in most things.

Heartlanders

Older traditionalists, they want plain-vanilla houses. They reject Winners' greed and ambition.

Authenticks

Above-average income, high education. They are against status and display. They want outdoor living room, to be close to nature.

well-written and nonpejorative, whereas the descriptions of the other segments can hardly be described as positive.

Third, in 1994, the segment was revealed only to the interviewer on a one-on-one basis; in 2003, although there was no necessity for any individual to mention which Tribe he or she was in, it became public very quickly—and the negative slant in the descriptions of some of the Tribes played out in an interesting manner. No one wanted to be seen as an Upkeeper (the very name is problematic and has since been changed); these were the people who insisted that they saw themselves in at least two of the groups.

Cahill and Polansky (1997) called for further research on the subject of exposing a typology to consumers; this project did so with quite different results. Clearly a need exists for further research into the issue of the willingness of consumers to be typecast into segments in a typology. One specific question that needs to be answered is whether the willingness to be typologized is related to the pain of the search and purchase processes; specifically, Cahill and Polansky (1997) found that the willingness of their respondents seemed to be related to the painful process of buying real estate. Would they be so willing if it were for toothpaste?

Pending the further research, it seems clear that exposing customers to a typology is like making sausage in public: inadvisable. The negativity of the focus-group members' reactions grew as they fed off each other's responses, finally ending in a place where no marketer wants customers to be—they were almost angry. There is another way out of this problem, particularly if customers are interactively working with computers: the Amazon.com approach. When one logs on to Amazon.com and requests a book title, immediately below that listing is the statement that "people who bought [whatever book] also are interested in these books," presenting one or more books on the same topic. Taking the real estate market as the case, it would be possible to have an individual either self-select a Tribe or take the Tribes instrument (but not have the computer tell the individual which Tribe he or she belongs to) and say that "people who looked at this house also liked these houses."

THOUGHT TWO

Another issue concerning segmentation is whether to segment or not, and, if the answer is yes, how much. Given that I have written this book and a previous book on segmentation, it should be obvious that I generally approve of segmentation.

A golden age of mass marketing never existed—not even in the 1950s. Not everyone watched *Leave It to Beaver*, or used Tide, or drove Chevrolets. In the 1950s, there were more than six American car manufacturers, three television and four radio networks, and several manufacturers of soap powders. Furthermore, although the post–World War II expansion created several Levittowns, not everyone moved into them or wanted to. Older, existing suburbs managed to grow in the face of the new suburbs. In short, there were choices for consumers at every point in their consumption experience. This may not have been "Marketing 1:1," but I have never been overly impressed with that concept; it did offer consumers a level of choice that was acceptable at the time.

Segmenting a market is not free. There are costs of performing the research, fielding surveys and focus groups, designing multiple packages, and designing multiple advertisements and communications messages. The goal, of course, is to ensure that by segmenting the market, by aiming products and packages and communications tailored for specific groups at those specific groups, that sales will increase. They have to increase by more than the costs involved, of course, before it is a worthwhile endeavor. How much does all the "segmentation costs" add up to? It can vary greatly, but, for a product with a national reach, a national survey and the focus groups "required" to surface the right questions to field and perhaps a pretest of the survey to ensure that those being surveyed answer the questions you are asking with answers that you are looking for are called for.[3] Having fielded the survey and designed the segments, there are costs attendant with getting everyone up to speed with what the segments are, who is in them, and how to reach them. Then the advertisements must be written (and filmed if they are for television), packages designed, and everything assembled. There will be additional warehouse costs, as the number of different packages must be stored in smaller numbers than "one size fits all." What does all of this add up to? Focus groups can be had for somewhere under $10,000 for two. The last national survey I was involved with cost $20,000 in direct costs to write, print, and mail (including return postage); scoring was another $10,000. This survey did not involve segmenting; the last segmentation study I was involved with cost around $50,000 for the statistics of segmentation. Additional package design, writing more than one advertisement, etc., would add more money, as will the training needed to teach everyone in the organization the new scheme. In short, it will cost around $200,000 to $250,000 to do a product segmentation.[4] Given the realities of profit margins, this large a cost is going to take a several-million-dollar increase in sales to recoup (although some of the costs are one-time costs, others are annual costs).

The fiscal realities of this analysis dictate some segmentation realities.

1. Unless you expect an upsurge in sales because of the segmentation, don't segment.

2. If you are planning a fad or near-fad product, don't segment; the amount of time may be more important than the cost, and segmenting also takes time.

3. After performing the studies, you may realize that your product will only appeal to one or two segments. Do not feel that you have to sell into each segment in order to be successful; often, knowing where *not* to sell is as important and as profitable as knowing where to sell. Designing a campaign that targets one or two segments and ignores the others will also reduce costs, because the amount of packaging and advertising costs will be reduced.

4. Do the least you can. If demographic segmentation will work for your product or service, the use demographic segmentation. If geographic segmentation will work because your product will only appeal to people in a certain region, then use it. Just because psychographic segmentation is sexier and more sophisticated than demographics or geographic segmentation does not make it better. Better is what works for your product or service at the least possible cost.

REVIEW QUESTION

1. Would you be willing to be segmented by marketers to make buying a product easier? To make it unnecessary to listen to communications for products you have no intention of buying? Why or why not?

Appendix

Perceptual Mapping

Perceptual mapping is a technique used to graphically represent the position of a particular offering in terms of the other offerings in a specific category of products or services. There are generally two goals when managers use perceptual maps. The first is to determine where the firm's offering is positioned with respect to those of the competition. Second is to help identify product or service attributes that are important to customers and that can be used to differentiate one's offerings from others. No matter how important a particular attribute may be in the customer's mind, unless the customer perceives differences across offerings, that attribute will not be influential in the customer's decisions when chosing among alternatives. Frequently the attributes that are important to customers are latent and unobservable (or, more usually, are deemed unimportant) by management; perceptual mapping helps in the essential task of uncovering these latent dimensions and making them and their importance apparent to all concerned. As is so often the case, and as I have often mentioned in this book and elsewhere, managers tend not to belong to the target group(s), so what is obvious to the group is often missed by the managers and vice versa.

Why make perceptual maps? Very simply, because it is often easier for people to see and understand relationships when they are presented graphically rather than in columns of figures or long verbal descriptions. The various techniques of perceptual mapping all deliver as their final product a graphic map of the various attributes, locating the different offerings already in the marketplace in space with relation to each other and with relation to the various attributes uncovered by quantitative surveying of customers and potential customers. The numbers used to create the maps can be presented to managers in tabular form, but they are easier to interpret

---

This appendix is a simplification of the material presented in Chapter 3 of Cahill, 1995a.

when presented graphically. Whose perceptual maps should be used? The easy and obvious answer is the potential customers'. However, this is only part of the answer. The offering firm's management personnel have perceptions that may or may not be congruent with those of their customers. Laying the two sets of maps atop each other could be a beneficial exercise, as management has a tendency to impose its will and its perceptions upon the products to be offered.

Why is perceptual mapping not used more in new-product introductions? The biggest impediment seems to be that the research necessary to produce the maps needs to be done early in the design process, and this is precisely the time when firms are the most distracted. Also, perceptual mapping is not free. It certainly costs less to produce than a segmentation scheme, although, to realize the full benefits of the maps, a segmentation scheme should already be in place. I think part of the problem with mapping is that it is not a "sexy" technique; when done well, it is almost too easy to see what should be done, and therefore there is little room for a consultant to pontificate.

How to make the maps? There are three basic techniques: factor analysis, discriminant analysis, and multidimensional scaling. Each has its uses and advocates. Kohli and Leuthesser (1993) outlined these three techniques for managers, compared their strengths and weaknesses, and described when to use each. Much of the following discussion is based on this article combined with other material and stripped of academese and made as application oriented as possible.

Factor Analysis is essentially a data-reduction technique in which the objective is to represent the original assembly of a large number of attributes in terms of a smaller number of underlying dimensions or factors. After the factors have been identified, the brands' ratings on these factors are used to position the brands on the map. The first step is to produce "Factor Loadings," which are roughly analogous to a set of correlation statistics. Each factor loading is a measure of the importance of the variable when measuring each factor. The "explanation of variance" in the variable is displayed numerically in the Factor-Loading Table as a single statistic, analogous to the R^2 in multiple regressions. After all of this statistical work is completed, it is possible to take the data points and plot them in a graph, thus showing graphically where each of the offerings lies.

Cluster Analysis may be used to identify offerings that are similar along some criteria. As a technique, it is less sophisticated than factor analysis, but, in return for this, it is easier to perform. The purpose of cluster analysis is to group offerings into a small number of mutually exclusive groupings with quite similar characteristics so that they may be discussed as if they were a single offering. It is a technique that is frequently employed in market segmentation.

Discriminant Analysis is also used to reduce the number of attributes to a smaller number of underlying dimensions. However, discriminant analysis focuses on the attributes that show differences among offerings, unlike cluster analysis, which focuses on their similarities. Discriminant Analysis tends to ignore attribute ratings that show large variations within offerings and focuses instead on attribute ratings that show large variation among offerings—or between one respondent and another. A major difference in the method of presentation is that in the perceptual maps prepared from discriminant analysis it is possible to assess how strong the agreement among respondents is on one factor in relation to other factors.

In their comparison of factor analysis and discriminant analysis, Kohli and Leuthesser (1993, p. 18) give a roadmap of when to use each. Discriminant analysis should be preferred when there are objective dimensions to measure. The two techniques can be used complementarily to highlight substantial differences in agreement among consumers. Furthermore, factor analysis should be preferred when there are few offerings in a category. Given these conditions, factor analysis will be preferred over discriminant analysis much of the time if for no other reason than that there are usually few objectively determinable dimensions that are important to the consumer.

Multidimensional Scaling (MDS) maps the offerings spatially so that their relative positions in the mapped space reflects the degree of perceived similarity among them. Respondents evaluate the offerings in pairs—either in rank order or by rating—judging the overall similarity between the paired offerings. Unlike either factor analysis or discriminant analysis, MDS asks respondents to rate offerings on overall similarity, not individual attributes.

Kohli and Leuthesser (1993, pp. 15-16) suggest some considerations in making the decision of which technique to use. First, MDS works better the large the number of offerings available for respondents; in markets where there are only a few offerings, MDS loses power. Offsetting this desirability of large numbers of offerings is the fact that the larger the number, the more complex the raking or rating job facing respondents, calling into question some of the real-world validity of the results. Second, MDS requires only similarity judgments for the pairings; therefore, it is not necessary to do prior research to determine which attributes are important in consumer choice. Thus, when it is not clear that the relevant attributes can be specified for respondents, MDS is preferable. There are relatively few research firms that use these techniques as rather standard tools in their kit; most firms do not use them at all. It seems that firms that do use them, use them frequently. Most marketing PhDs are able to the quantitative and interpretive work involved, so finding a researcher to produce and interpret the maps should not be a problem in most communities.

Am I claiming too much for perceptual maps? After all, if they are so good and powerful and easy to produce and interpret, why do so few firms use them? This is a valid question. Part of the answer lies in the fact that performing the research and analysis costs money; if one is dealing with a new product or service, this money needs to be spent in the development phase—a time when corporate resources are usually relatively stretched.

Notes

Preface

1. I picked the title of *How Consumers Pick a Hotel* carefully, not expecting anyone would think it was a book designed only for people running hotels. To my mind it was an explicitly consumer-behavior book; this one is not.

Chapter 1

1. Although I am generally prone to segment, there is always the danger that segmenting a market and designing the communications strategies for the various segments will cost more than the increase in efficiency and effectiveness and profitability to the firm. In such cases, the countervailing wisdom is, in fact, correct.

2. There are few books about business-to-business marketing. Weinstein (2004) and Bonoma and Shapiro (1983) are the best available. The chapter on industrial segmentation in *How Consumers Pick a Hotel* certainly is shorter, but it has put at least two people I know soundly to sleep.

Chapter 6

1. See Cahill (1997, pp. 66-67) for the citations to LOV and Kahle's ongoing work.

Chapter 7

1. There is no real reason to expect that liking an ad is going to encourage one to purchase a product, even if a negative attitude toward an ad might discourage one from buying the product. "Liking" an ad may encourage, rather, someone knowing and watching the ads just for their content; the infamous watching of the Super Bowl for the ads rather than the football game is an example of this behavior. I remember a lunch when I worked at Wyse Advertising when three of us who all grew up in the 1950s and all watched lots of children's television were together. We were all able to sing jingles for many, many products advertised on those programs—verbatim, even after forty years of life's going by. Like the ads? We all agreed they were appalling in retrospect, and weren't much better then, but we knew the products, knew the advertisements.

Chapter 9

1. The kiosk was called InfoVision and is discussed in detail in Cahill (1995a) and Hisrich and Cahill (1995).

2. Wyse produced an advertisement for Creata-Card at the very beginning of its life in which a little boy has broken a lamp and he and his father go to the store and make a "Mommy, I'm sorry I broke your lamp" card. They got around the difficulty of the height of the kiosk by having the boy sit on his father's shoulders. It was the most effective ad I have seen in years for any product; I was told by people at the agency that there was literally hardly a dry eye in the room—filled with hard-boiled agency and client employees—when the ad was screened.

3. I find the statistic for "their own money" high for the younger end of the market, and for teenage boys to spend a "major portion" of their money on clothing is simply unbelievable.

4. The idiocy of such a statement is highlighted in the same OnLine NewsHour piece (Harper, 2004) stating that NASCAR is a major player in the placement market. In early 2004 one of the drivers accepted sponsorship by the movie *The Passion of the Christ*—a somewhat controversial movie. If the distributors of the movie thought that only the 200,000 or so people who were actually at the track the week the car had the ad on the hood would see the ad—and could see the ad as the car whizzed around at speeds in excess of 150 mph—I doubt the distributors would have paid to paint the hood. They were undoubtedly expecting several million people to turn on their televisions and watch the race there, where the cameras focus on the cars for lengthy periods of time, stopping their apparent motion and making the sponsors' logos visible.

Chapter 12

1. The fact that this tribe has had three names in the space of less than fifteen years shows some of the problems inherent in naming segments. The original "Wannabes"—an offshoot from the VALS Type "Emulators"—was obviously negative and sneering. "Upkeepers" seemed to offer a more neutral term but was recently replaced by "Self-Sufficient," which at least has positive connotations. I have written elsewhere about DCI's tendency to change the names of its products and the confusion that it sometimes causes both internally and externally (Cahill, 1995b).

2. Actually, this statement is true of everyone, not just Authenticks. There are two streams of research that deal directly with this point. The first is a book, now more than twenty years old, that described the research done in Chicago by interviewers going into people's houses and asking them to discuss their possessions, particularly the ones in their living rooms (Csikszentmihalyi and Rochberg-Halton, 1981). All the possessions so described were freighted with symbol and value and meaning far beyond their physicality. The second stream of research is typified by Clare Cooper Marcus (1976), who wrote that one's house is a physical symbol of one's psychological self. Lest this seem terribly abstruse for a marketing book, this treatment of houses also appears in many works of American fiction (Chandler, 1991). Triangulating this research in these multiple disciplines makes it quite apparent how important houses are to people (Cahill, 1994).

Chapter 13

1. These authors did not cite the Csikszentmihalyi and Rochberg-Halton (1981) work, but it so starkly parallels that work that it is almost eerie.

2. In this the American LIVES respondents were no different from the respondents of every survey or focus group on residential real estate that I have been associated with over the past twenty years. Real estate agents are held in very low repute as information sources; people feel that real estate agents distort and withhold information, acting counter to the interests of everyone in the transaction process.

3. Although statistically the matching was secure, that the analysis was conducted only in Denver, a city with few remaining "older" houses, meant that the house types were significantly skewed to new construction, a fact that was redoubled by the fact that American LIVES had worked, and continues to work, very extensively with builders. The results would undoubtedly be different in other cities that have significantly larger numbers of existing houses that are still seen as desirable.

Chapter 14

1. The VIN on an automobile is far more than merely a serial or identifying number; it contains coded information about factory-installed equipment such as the motor, transmission, some features and—in recent years—a color code. If AutoAd could accept the VIN as input (much as ReAd does with Multiple Listing Service data), much data would not need to be input manually, thus answering the complaint that the used-car managers had voiced in their focus group in 1989 and answering an ongoing complaint from real estate agents about double work. The search for what one of my friends calls the "Captain Midnight VIN-decoder ring" has become a combination of the Arthurian search for the Holy Grail and Captain Ahab's quest for the Great White Whale. A lot of time and energy has been expended for no result. The decoders exist, but there is something wrong for AutoAd's use with each and every one, either in price to AutoAd for using the decoder or the fact that some of them extract too little data from the VIN for ad-writing purposes, because they are designed for other reasons.

2. The Appendix contains a technical but nonquantitative discussion of perceptual maps and their uses.

Chapter 15

1. I have always considered the popularity of Neapolitan ice cream to be at least a partial refutation of this bit of parental wisdom.

2. In the past couple of years the requirements to earn the Merit Badge have changed from an almost-total emphasis on cooking while camping out—which makes sense given the Boy Scouts' emphasis on camping—to having a requirement that the Scout has made several meals at home prior to the cooking on campouts. As a counselor for the Cooking Merit Badge, I can attest to the fact that more and more of the boys who try to earn the badge fall afoul of this requirement, as they have

never cooked at home (microwaving food does not count) and were hoping to learn to cook from me at camp.

3. The people at SRI International found the same dichotomy between Achievers and the Societally Conscious long before we were using the Tribes scheme and pointed the dichotomy out to us on more than one occasion.

Chapter 16

1. Anyone with an interest in this field will find much to become ill over—Upton Sinclair's *The Jungle* is often enough to put one off lunch. However, the titles of the histories of nineteenth-century patent medicines appeal to the historian's somewhat-twisted sense of humor, such as *Toadstool Millionaires* and *One If for a Man, Six If for a Horse*. Dosage was uncertain, at best; "the amount of calomel that will fit on a broad knife-blade" was often suggested for a laxative. Calomel is a mercury compound, highly irritating to the bowel, and lethal in its effect if overused, which it frequently was.

2. The *Proceedings of the Association for Consumer Research* and the *Journal of Consumer Research* contain papers and articles almost every year on the subject of using marketing and consumer science techniques to help reduce harmful behaviors, but there seems to be neither a meta-analysis of this material nor much building upon previous work by any of the studies.

Chapter 17

1. This particular client talks his way through all of his thinking—he bounces ideas off people who work for him or who happen to be at a party with him. It took me several years to realize this was part of his character; it drove me to distraction then, but I am now much more relaxed about it. I simply refuse to pay attention to the proceedings until he has more or less made up his mind about a subject.

Chapter 18

1. In addition to being sexist and always discussed in terms of the "typical blue-collar marriage"—implying, of course, that at best the woman would be belittled as Archie Bunker was forever belittling Edith in *All in the Family,* which aired at the time, and at worst beaten—the story totally ignored the reality of mutual brand choice, which was never discussed as a possibility. Women were seen as not being beer drinkers, even in a college setting, where the few women who were enrolled in business schools at the time probably *were* beer drinkers.

Chapter 19

1. There is a television ad being currently aired where some of the people being "interviewed" don't know the names of the parts of the house, such as gable. Be-

cause the intent is for people to hire a realtor, one expects the actors not to "know" terms such as "contingency clause."

2. There was no attempt in this research project to find out which of the different VALS types would be comfortable living on the same block with each other. Given some of the remarks made at the focus groups held to discuss the Tribes scheme, it would seem that they not only would be, but have expectations that they would be, living with other groups—at least those who live in older, more-established communities.

3. Survey questions can frequently run afoul of the "I know you think you know what I meant, but I am not sure that I meant what you said" problems. Pretests are always good if there is any serious sophistication required for answering.

4. Service segmentation is also expensive but of course does not bear the cost of designing and producing multiple packages or warehousing.

References

AARP (1999). "Baby Boomers Envision Their Retirement: An AARP Segmentation Analysis." Washington, DC. Available on the Internet at research/aarp.org/econ/boomer_seg_prn.html.

Alving, Barbara (2004). "The Increasing Number of Adults with High Blood Pressure Statement." *NIH News* (August 23) Available on the Internet at www.nih.gov/news/pr/aug2004/nhlbi-23.htm.

American LIVES (1991). *Study of the Denver Real Estate Market.* San Francisco, CA.

Archambeault, Bill (2004). "'Tween Angst: B*tween Productions Targets Market, Needs for Girls Ages 9-13." *Boston Business Journal* (July 26). Available on the Internet at boston.bizjournals.com/boston/stories/2004/07/26/smallb1.html.

Atlas, James (1984). "Beyond Demographics." *Atlantic Monthly* (October), pp. 49-58.

Ball, Deborah, Sarah Ellison, Janet Adamy, and Geoffrey A. Fowler (2004). "Recipes Without Borders?" *The Wall Street Journal* (August 18), pp. B1, B3.

Beatty, Sally Goll (1995). "Women's Views of Their Lives Aren't Reflected by Advertisers." *The Wall Street Journal* (December 19), p. B6.

Belk, Russell W., Guliz Ger, and Soren Askegaard (2000). "The Missing Streetcar Named Desire." In S. Ratneshwar, David Glen Mick, and Cynthia Huffman (eds.), *The Why of Consumption: Contemporary Perspectives on Consumer Motives, Goals, and Desires* (pp. 98-119). London: Routledge.

Bellah, Robert N., Richard Madsen, William M. Sullivan, Ann Swidler, and Steven M. Tipton (1985). *Habits of the Heart: Individualism and Commitment in American Life.* New York: Harper & Row.

Bikson, Tora K., Barbara A. Gutek, and Don A. Mankin (1981). *Implementation of Information Technology in Office Settings: Review of Relevant Literature.* Santa Monica, CA: The Rand Corp, P-6697.

Bonoma, Thomas V. and Benson P. Shapiro (1983). *Segmenting the Industrial Market.* Lexington, MA: Lexington Books.

Brunton, David (1987). "600 Hear Theories on How Boomers Act As Consumers." *Cleveland Plain Dealer* (November 17), p. 2-E.

Bruskin-Goldring Research (1997). *The 1997 Auto Remarketing Study. Decision-Making: New vs Used.* Princeton, NJ.

Bryant, Barbara (1986). The Market Segmentation Cake: Survey Research Batter with Lifestyle Frosting. Paper presented at Managing Consumer Change, February 12-14, Hollywood, FL.

Buss, Dale (2004). "Is the Food Industry the Problem or the Solution?" *The New York Times,* August 29. Available on the Internet at www.NYTimes.com.

Buzzell, Robert D. and Michael J. Baker (1972). "Sales Effectiveness of Automobile Advertising." *Journal of Advertising Research,* vol. 12 (June), pp. 3-8.

Cadwallader, Eva H. (1980). "The Main Features of Value Experience." *Journal of Value Inquiry,* vol. 14, pp. 229-244.

Cahill, Dennis J. (1994). "Does Your House Look Like Your Dog?" *Environment and Behavior,* vol. 26, no. 5 (September), pp. 698-703.

———. (1995a). *Squeezing a New Service into a Crowded Market.* Binghamton, NY: The Haworth Press.

———. (1995b). "We Sure As Hell Confused Ourselves, But What About the Customers?" *Marketing Intelligence and Planning,* vol. 13, no. 4, pp. 5-9.

———. (1996). *Internal Marketing: Your Company's Next Stage of Growth.* Binghamton, NY: The Haworth Press.

———. (1997) *How Consumers Pick a Hotel: Strategic Segmentation and Target Marketing.* Binghamton, NY: The Haworth Press.

Cahill, Dennis, J. and Sharon H. Polansky (1997). "Exploring a House-Buying Typology: A Case Study of Qualitative Segmentation." *Journal of Segmentation in Marketing,* vol. 1, no. 2, pp. 93-101.

Camacho, Frank E. and Diane Schmalensee (1989). Why It's So Difficult to See the Effects of Attitudes on Sales. Paper presented at the American Marketing Association Attitude Research Conference, January 29-February 1.

Campbell, Colin (1987). *The Romantic Ethic and the Spirit of Modern Consumerism.* London: Basil Blackwell.

———. (1997). "*The Romantic Ethic and the Spirit of Modern Consumerism:* Reflections on the Reception of a Thesis Concerning the Origin of the Continuing Desire for Goods." In Susan M. Pearce (ed.), *Experiencing Material Culture in the Western World* (pp. 36-48). London: Leicester University Press.

Chandler, Marilyn R. (1991). *Dwelling in the Text: Houses in American Fiction.* Berkeley: University of California Press.

Cho, Janet H. (2004). "American Greetings' Line Targets 6- to 12-Year-Old Consumer." *Cleveland Plain Dealer* (July 17), pp. C1, C3.

Claxton, Reid P. (1995). "Birth Order As a Market Segmentation Variable." *Journal of Consumer Marketing,* vol. 12, no. 3, pp. 22-38.

Cooper [Marcus], Clare (1976). "The House As Symbol of the Self." In H. Proshansky, W. Ittelson, and L. Rivlin (eds.), *Environmental Psychology,* Second Edition (pp. 435-448). New York: Holt, Rinehart & Winston.

———. (1978). "Remembrances of Landscapes Past." *Landscape,* vol. 22, no. 3, pp. 178-195.

Csikszentmihalyi, Mihalyi and Eugene Rochberg-Halton (1981). *The Meaning of Things: Domestic Symbols and the Self.* Cambridge: University of Cambridge Press.

Demby, Emanuel (1974). "Psychographics and from Whence It Came." In William D. Wells (ed.), *Life Style and Psychographics* (pp. 11-30). Chicago, IL: American Marketing Association.

————. (1989). "Psychographics Revisited: The Birth of a Technique." *Marketing News* (January), p. 21.

DeSarbo, Wayne S. and Christian F. DeSarbo (2003). "A Generalized Normative Segmentation Methodology Employing Conjoint Analysis." In Anders Gustafson, Andreas Herrmann, and Frank Huber (eds.), *Conjoint Measurement: Methods and Applications,* Third Edition (pp. 473-504). Berlin: Springer-Verlag.

Dreyfus, Ira (2004). "Panel Offers Food Pyramid Changes." *Cleveland Plain Dealer* (August 28), p. A2.

Dubisch, Jill (1981). "You Are What You Eat: Religious Aspects of the Health Food Movement." In W. Arens and Susan Montague (eds.), *The American Dimension: Cultural Myths and Social Realities,* Second Edition (pp. 115-127). Sherman Oaks, CA: Alfred Publishing Co., Inc.

Englis, Basil G. and Michael R. Solomon (1995). "To Be *and* Not to Be: Lifestyle Imaging, Reference Groups, and *The Clustering of America.*" *Journal of Advertising,* vol. 24, no. 1 (Spring), pp. 13-28.

Fallowes, James (2004). "How Google Took the Work Out of Selling Advertising." *The New York Times* (June 13). Available on the Internet at www.NYTimes.com.

Farley, John U., Jerrold Katz, and Donald R. Lehmann (1978). "Impact of Different Comparison Sets on Evaluation of a New Subcompact Car Brand." *Journal of Consumer Research,* vol. 5 (September), pp. 138-142.

Fennell, Geraldine, Greg M. Allenby, Sha Yang, and Yancy Edwards (2003). "The Effectiveness of Demographic and Psychographic Variables for Explaining Brand and Product Category Use." *Quantitative Marketing and Economics,* vol. 1, pp. 223-244.

Ferrell, O. C. (1985). "Implementing and Monitoring Ethics in Advertising." In Gene R. Laczniak and Patrick E. Murphy (eds.), *Marketing Ethics: Guidelines for Managers* (pp. 27-40). Lexington, MA: Lexington Books.

Fiffer, Sharon Sloan and Steve Fiffer (eds.) (1995). *Home: American Writers Remember Rooms of Their Own.* New York: Pantheon Books.

Fischer, David Hackett (1989). *Albion's Seed: Four British Folkways in America.* New York: Oxford University Press.

Fournier, Susan and Michael Guiry (1993). "An Emerald Green Jaguar, a House on Nantucket, and an African Safari: Wish Lists and Consumption Dreams in Materialist Society." In Leigh McAllister and Michael L. Rothschild (eds.), *Advances in Consumer Research,* vol. 20 (pp. 352-358). Provo, UT: Association for Consumer Research.

Francese, Peter (2001). "Big Spenders." *American Demographics* (September), pp. 30-31.

Francese, Peter (2002). "Trend Ticker: Older and Wealthier." *American Demographics* (November), pp. 40-41.

Freudenheim, Betty (1988). "Who Lives Here, Go-Getter or Grouch?" *The New York Times* (March 31), p. 16.

Gates, Michael (1989). "VALS Changes with the Times." *Incentive* (June), pp. 27-30, 73.

Goodwin, Cathy and Larry Lockshin (1992). "The Solo Consumer: Unique Opportunity for the Service Marketer." *Journal of Services Marketing,* vol. 6, no. 3 (Summer), pp. 27-36.

Greene, Kelly (2004). "Marketing Surprise: Older Consumers Buy Stuff, Too." *The Wall Street Journal* (April 6), pp. A1, A12.

Hagerty, James R. (2004). "As Home Sales Cool, Ranks of Realtors Grow Crowded." *The Wall Street Journal,* January 20, pp. A1, A6.

Hagerty, James R. and Queena Sook Kim (2004). "Luxury Home for Sale: 6 Bdrms, Dumpster Vu." *The Wall Street Journal* (August 5), pp. D1, D2.

Halpern, Michelle (2004). "Cute, but Scary." *Marketing Magazine* (August 9). Available on the Internet at www.marketingmag.ca/magazine/current/feature/article.jsp?content=20040809_628.

Hammer, Allen L. and Wayne D. Mitchell (1996). "The Distribution of MBTI Types in the US by Gender and Ethnic Group." *Journal of Psychological Type,* vol. 37, pp. 2-15.

Harper, Liz (2004). Online NewsHour Extra (July). Available on the Internet at www.PBS.org.

Hawkins, Lee, Jr. (2004). "GM Launches Print Campaign to Sell More Autos to Blacks." *The Wall Street Journal* (August 10), p. B8.

Hisrich, Robert D. and Dennis J. Cahill (1995). "Buried at the Crossroads at Midnight with an Oak Stake Through Its Heart: An Entrepreneurial Replication of Ross and Staw's Extended Temporal Escalation Model." *Family Business Review,* vol. 8, no. 1, pp. 41-54.

Holden, Stephen J. S. and Richard J. Lutz (1992). "Ask Not What the Brand Can Evoke; Ask What Can Evoke the Brand?" In *Advances in Consumer Research,* vol. 19 (pp. 101-107).

Hollander, John (1993). "It All Depends." In Arlen Mack (ed.), *Home: A Place in the World.* New York: University Press.

Holt, Douglas B. (1995). "How Consumers Consume: A Typology of Consumption Practices." *Journal of Consumer Research,* vol. 22 (June), pp. 1-16.

———. (1997). "Poststructuralist Lifestyle Analysis: Conceptualizing the Social Patterning of Consumption in Postmodernity," *Journal of Consumer Research,* vol. 23 (March), pp. 326-350.

Holt, Douglas B. and Julient B. Schor (2000). "Introduction." In Juliet B. Schor and Douglas B. Holt (eds.), *The Consumer Society Reader* (pp. vii-xxiii). New York: The New Press.

Institute of Healthcare Improvement Newsletter (2002). "One Size Does Not Fit All—Think Segmentation." (April.) Available on the Internet at www.path institute.com.

Johnson, KerenAnn and Scott D. Roberts (1992). "Incompletely-Launched and Returning Young Adults: Social Change, Consumption, and Family Environment." In Robert P. Leone and V. Kumar (eds.), *1992 AMA Educators' Proceedings* (pp. 249-254). Chicago, IL: American Marketing Associations.

Kahle, Lynn R. (ed.) (1983). *Social Values and Social Change: Adaptation to Life in America.* New York: Praeger.

Kahle, Lynn R., Sharon E. Beatty, and Pamela Homer (1986). "Alternative Measurement Approaches to Customer Values: The List of Values (LOV) and Values and Life Style (VALS)." *Journal of Consumer Research,* vol. 13 (December), pp. 405-409.

Kamakura, Wagner A. and Jose Afonso Mazzon (1991). "Value Segmentation: A Model for the Measurement of Values and Value Systems." *Journal of Consumer Research,* vol. 18 (September), pp. 208-218.

Kamakura, Wagner A. and Thomas P. Novak (1992). "Value-System Segmentation: Exploring the Meaning of LOV." Journal of Consumer Research, vol. 19, pp. 119-132

Kang, Stephanie (2004). "All Wet? Retailer Calls in Teen 'Stylizers' to Revive Sales." *The Wall Street Journal* (July 30), pp. B1, B2.

Kaufman, Carol Felker (1995). "Shop 'Til You Drop: Tales from a Physically Challenged Shopper." *Journal of Consumer Marketing,* vol. 12, no. 3, pp. 39-55.

Kelman, Herbert C. (1980). "The Role of Action in Attitude Change." In Monte M. Page (ed.), *Beliefs, Attitudes, and Values: Nebraska Symposium on Motivation, 1979* (pp. 117-194). Lincoln, NE: University of Nebraska Press.

Kiersey, David (1989). *Portraits of Temperament.* Del Mar, CA: Prometheus Nemesis Book.

Kiersey, David and Marilyn Bates (1984). *Please Understand Me: Character & Temperament Types.* Del Mar, CA: Prometheus Nemesis Book.

Kim, Queena Sook and Suzanne Vranica (2004). "'Tween Queen Comes to Fashion Doll's Aid." *The Wall Street Journal* (August 23), pp. B1, B3.

Kohli, Chiranjeev S. and Lance Leuthesser (1993). "Product Positioning: A Comparison of Perceptual Mapping Techniques." *Journal of Product and Brand Management,* vol. 2, no. 4, pp. 10-19.

Lastovicka, John L. (1982). "On the Validation of Lifestyle Traits: A Review and Illustration." *Journal of Marketing Research,* vol. 20 (February), pp. 126-138.

Lawrence, Gordon (1982). *People Types and Tiger Stripes: A Practical Guide to Learning Styles,* Second Edition. Palo Alto, CA: Consulting Psychologists Press.

Lee, Keun S. and Paul J. Hensel (1990). "Conceptual and Methodological Issues in Contemporary Values Research in Consumer Behavior: A Critical Analysis." In B. J. Dunlap (ed.), *Developments in Marketing Science, XIII* (pp. 30-34). Cullowhee, NC: Academy of Marketing Science.

Leeming, E. Janice and Cynthia F. Tripp (1994). *Segmenting the Women's Market.* Chicago, IL: Probus Publishing, Inc.

Lesser, Jack A. and Marie Adele Hughes (1986). "The Generalizability of Psychographic Market Segments Across Geographic Locations." *Journal of Marketing,* vol. 50 (January), pp. 18-27.

Lipton, Laura (2004). "Back to School: It's Not About the Clothes." *The Wall Street Journal* (August 27), pp. W1, W4.

Littlefield, James E., Yeqing Bao, and Don L. Cook (2000). "Internet Real Estate Information: Are Home Purchasers Paying Attention to It?" *Journal of Consumer Marketing,* vol. 17, no. 7, pp. 575-590.

Lofland, Laurie and Nabil Y. Razzouk (1992). "Revisiting the Family Life Cycle: Modifications and Implications." In Victoria L. Crittenden (ed.), *Developments in Marketing Science,* Volume 15 (pp. 43-47). Chesnut Hill, MA: Academy of Marketing Science.

Malcolm, Andrew H. (1987). "Teen-Age Shoppers: Desperately Seeking Spinach." *The New York Times* (November 29), p. 10F.

Marcus, Clare Cooper (1995). *House As a Mirror of Self: Exploring the Deeper Meaning of Home.* Berkeley, CA: Conari Press.

McCracken, Grant (1986). "Culture and Consumption: A Theoretical Account of the Structure and Movement of the Cultural Meaning of Consumer Goods." *Journal of Consumer Research,* vol. 13 (June), pp. 71-84.

———. (1988). *Culture and Consumption: New Approaches to the Symbolic Character of Consumer Goods and Activities.* Bloomington, IN: Indiana University Press.

Merenski, J. Paul (1981). "Psychographics: Valid by Definition and Reliable by Technique." In Venkatakrishna V. Bellur (ed.), *Developments in Marketing Science,* Volume IV (pp. 161-166). Muncie, IN: Academy of Marketing Science.

Miles, Steven (2002). "Consuming Youth, Consuming Lifestyles." In Steven Miles, Alison Anderson, and Kevin Meethan (eds.), *The Changing Consumer: Markets and Meanings* (pp. 131-144). London: Routledge.

Mills, Stephen J. (1988). *Participatory Health: VALS and Consumer Health Attitudes and Behavior.* Menlo Park, CA: SRI International.

Mitchell, Arnold (1983). *The Nine American Lifestyles: Who We Are and Where We're Going.* New York: Warner Books.

———. (1984). *The Marrieds: Patterns, Attitudes, and Decision-Making of the VALS Marrieds.* Menlo Park, CA: SRI International.

Mitchell, Vincent-Wayne (1994a). "How to Identify Psychographic Segments: Part 1." *Marketing Intelligence & Planning,* vol. 12, no. 7, pp. 4-10.

———. (1994b). "How to Identify Psychographic Segments: Part 2." *Marketing Intelligence & Planning,* vol. 12, no. 7, pp. 11-17.

Morgan, Carol M. and Doran J. Levy (1993). *Segmenting the Mature Market: Identifying, Targeting and Reaching America's Diverse, Booming Senior Markets.* Chicago: Probus Publishing Co.

————. (2002). *Marketing to the Mindset of Boomers and Their Elders: Using Psychographics and More to Identify and Reach Your Best Targets.* St. Paul, MN: AttitudeBase.

Munsch, Robert and Sheila McGraw (1997). *Love You Forever.* Buffalo, NY: Firefly Books.

Munsinger, Gary M., Jean E. Weber, and Richard W. Hansen (1975). "Joint Home Purchasing Decisions by Husbands and Wives." *Journal of Consumer Research,* vol. 1 (March), pp. 60-66.

Myers, Isabel Briggs and Mary H. McCaulley (1985). *Manual: A Guide to the Development and Use of the Myers-Briggs Type Indicator.* Palo Alto, CA: Consulting Psychologists Press.

Myers, Isabel Briggs and Peter B. Myers (1980). *Gifts Differing.* Palo Alto, CA: Consulting Psychologists Press.

Nasar, Jack L. (1988a). Architectural Symbolism: A Study of House-Style Meanings. Paper prepared for the Enviornmental Design Research Association Conference, Pomona, CA.

————. (1988b). Letter to the author, June 24, 1988.

————. (1989). "Symbolic Meanings of House Styles." *Environment and Behavior,* vol. 21, no. 3 (May), pp. 235-257.

National Institutes of Health (2004). *Strategic Plan for NIH Obesity Research.* NIH Publication No. 04-5493. Bethesda, MD: NIH.

National Market Measures (1988). *Qualitative Research Results for Home Characterizations.*

————. (2003). *Research Results for New Home Buyers Search Engine Concept Test.*

Newspaper Association of America (1995). "Dealer Guide to Used Vehicle Consumers." New York: Newspaper Association of America.

Ostberg, Jacob (2002). "A Consumer Perspective on Healthy Foods: Untangling the Taken-for-Granted Categorization." In William J. Kehoe and John H. Lindgren, Jr. (eds.), *2002 AMA Educators' Proceedings* (pp. 89-96). Chicago, IL: American Marketing Association.

Paik, Felicia (1997). "'House of the Week': Traditional Styles Win Buyers." *Wall Street Journal* (March 21), p. B14.

Paul, Pamela (2001). "Getting Inside Gen Y." *American Demographics* (September), pp. 42-49.

Peppers, Don and Marsha Rogers (1993). *The One-to-One Future: Building Relationships One Customer at a Time.* New York: Currency-Doubleday.

Piirto, Rebecca (1990). "Measuring Minds in the 1990s." *American Demographics* (December), pp. 30-35.

————. (1991). *Beyond Mind Games: The Marketing Power of Psychographics.* New York: American Demographics Books.

Ploss, Kathryn (1987). *The VALS Types, 1987: Demographics, Attitudes, Consumption Patterns, Activities, and Media Usage.* Menlo Park, CA: SRI International.

Prakash, Ved and J. Michael Munson (1985). "Values, Expectations from the Marketing System and Product Expectations." *Psychology & Marketing,* vol. 2 (Winter), pp. 279-296.

Punj, Giris N. and Richard Staelin (1983). "A Model of Consumer Information Search Behavior for New Automobiles." *Journal of Consumer Research,* vol. 9 (March), pp. 366-380.

Regelson, Stanley (1981). "The Bagel: Symbol and Ritual at the Breakfast Table." In W. Arens and Susan P. Montague (eds.), *The American Dimension: Cultural Myths and Social Realities,* Second Edition (pp. 93-104). Sherman Oaks, CA: Alfred Publishing Co., Inc.

Reichl, Ruth (1998). *Tender at the Bone: Growing Up at the Table.* New York: Broadway Books.

———. (2001). *Comfort Me with Apples: More Adventures at the Table.* New York: Random House.

Rescher, Nicholas (1967). "The Study of Value Change." *Journal of Value Inquiry,* vol. 1, pp. 12-23.

Riche, Martha Farnsworth (1989). "Psychographics for the 1990s." *American Demographics* (July), pp. 24-26, 30-31, 53.

Riesman, David, Nathan Glazer, and Ruel Denny (1950/1961). *The Lonely Crowd.* New Haven, CT: Yale University Press.

Roberts, Scott D., Patricia K. Voli, and KerenAnn Johnson (1992). "Beyond the Family Life Cycle: An Inventory of Variables for Defining the Family as a Consumption Unit." In Victoria L. Crittenden (ed.), *Developments in Marketing Science,* Volume 15 (pp. 71-75). Chesnut Hill, MA: Academy of Marketing Science.

Rokeach, Milton (1968). *Beliefs, Attitudes, and Values: A Theory of Organization and Change.* San Francisco: Jossey-Bass, Inc.

———. (1968-1969). "The Role of Values in Public Opinion Research." *Public Opinion Quarterly,* vol. 35, no. 4 (Winter), pp. 547-559.

———. (1973). *The Nature of Human Values.* New York: The Free Press.

———. (1979). "From Individual to Institutional Values: With Special Reference to the Values of Science." In Milton Rokeach (ed.), *Understanding Human Values: Individual and Societal* (pp. 47-70). New York: The Free Press.

Rook, Dennis (1985). "The Ritual Dimension of Consumer Behavior." *Journal of Consumer Research,* vol. 12 (December), pp. 251-264.

Rundle, Rhonda L. (2004). "The Pitch Is Lifestyle: A Healthy One." *Wall Street Journal* (July 30), p. B3.

Sadalla, Edward K., Beth Vershure, and Jeffrey Burroughs (1987). "Identity Symbolism in Housing." *Environment and Behavior,* vol. 19, no. 5 (September), pp. 569-587.

Sayers, Dorothy L. (1933). *Murder Must Advertise.* London: Gollancz.

Scaninger, Charles M. and William D. Danko (1993). "A Conceptual and Empirical Comparison of Alternative Household Life Cycle Models." *Journal of Consumer Research,* vol. 19 (March), pp. 580-594.

Schor, Juliet B. and Douglas B. Holt (eds.) (2000). *The Consumer Society Reader.* New York: The New Press.

Schreiber, Alfred L. (2001). *Multicultural Marketing: Selling to the New America.* Chicago: NTC Books, Inc.

Schultz, Don (1994). "What Advertisers and Consumers Wanted in the Past, They Are Not Going to Want in the Future." *Link* (June), p. 44.

Sherif, Carolyn Wood (1980). "Social Values, Attitudes, and Involvement of the Self." In Monte M. Page (ed.), *Beliefs, Attitudes, and Values: Nebraska Symposium on Motivation, 1979* (pp. 1-64). Lincoln, NE: University of Nebraska Press.

Siegel, David L., Timothy J. Coffey, and Gregory Livingston (2001). *The Great Tween Buying Machine: Marketing to Today's Tweens.* Ithaca, NY: Paramount Market Publishing, Inc.

Simmons, Sid and Mark Esser (2003), "Developing Business Solutions from Conjoint Analysis." In Anders Gustafson, Andreas Herrmann, and Frank Huber (eds.), *Conjoint Measurement: Methods and Applications,* Third Edition (pp. 67-96). Berlin: Springer-Verlag.

Snyder, Robert (2002). "Mature Segmentation: Successfully Targeting the Mature Population." *Journal on Active Aging* (March-April), pp. 10-11, 49-50.

SRI International (1983). "American Portrait," a video.

Srinivasan, Harasimhan and Brian T. Ratchford (1991). "An Empircal Test of a Model of External Search for Automobiles." *Journal of Consumer Research,* vol. 18 (September), pp. 233-242.

Steingarten, Jeffrey (1997). *The Man Who Ate Everything.* New York: Vintage Books.

Straughan, Robert D. and James A. Roberts (1999). "Environmental Segmentation Alternatives: A Look at Green Consumer Behavior in the New Millennium." *Journal of Consumer Marketing,* vol.16, no. 6, pp. 558-575.

Sujan, Mita, James R. Bettman, and Hans Baumgartner (1993). "Influencing Consumer Judgments Using Autobiographical Memories: A Self-Referencing Perspective." *Journal of Marketing Research,* vol. 30, pp. 422-436.

Sukhdial, Ajay S., Goutam Chakraborty, and Eric K. Steger (1995). "Measuring Values Can Sharpen Segmentation in the Luxury Auto Market." *Journal of Advertising Research,* vol. 35 (January-February), pp. 9-22.

Susbauer, Jeffrey C., Dennis J. Cahill, Robert M. Warshawsky, and James Beckman (1994). "Culture Consulting in a Family-Owned Enterprise." *Small Business Institute Directors Association 1994 Conference Proceedings,* pp. 31-36, Lincoln, NE.

Swallow, Wendy (2004). *The Triumph of Love Over Experience: A Memoir of Remarriage.* New York: Hyperion.

Taylor, Lawrence (1981). "Coffee: The Bottomless Cup." In W. Arens and Susan Mantague (eds.), *The American Dimension: Cultural Myths and Social Realities,* Second Edition (pp. 107-112). Sherman Oaks, CA: Alfred Publishing Co., Inc.

Tian, Kelly Tepper, William O. Bearden, and Gary L. Hunter (2001). "Consumers' Need for Uniqueness: Scale Development and Validation." *Journal of Consumer Research*, vol. 28 (June), pp. 50-66.

Tinney, Cathie H. (1989). "Life Begins When the Kids Leave Home and the Dog Dies—But That's Where the Family Life Cycle Ends. In Jon M. Hawes and John Thanopolos (eds.), *Developments in Marketing Science*, Volume XII (pp. 59-63). Akron, OH: Academy of Marketing Science.

Townsend, Bickley (1985). "Psychographic Glitter and Gold." *American Demographics* (November), pp. 22-29, 32.

Trachtenberg, Jeffrey A. (2004). "Targeting Young Adults." *Wall Street Journal* (October 4), pp. B1, B5.

VALS (1989). *VALS 2 Consumer Segmentation for the 1990s*. Menlo Park, CA: SRI International.

Walker, Michael C. (2002) *Marketing to Seniors*. Bloomington, IN: 1st Books.

Wallendorf, Melanie and Eric J. Arnould (1991). "'We Gather Together': Consumption Rituals of Thanksgiving Day." *Journal of Consumer Marketing*, vol. 18 (June), pp. 13-31.

Warrick, Brooke H. (1984). *Intellectual and Emotional Styles of the VALS Types*. Menlo Park, CA: SRI International.

Wasson, Jeanie L. (1987). "Psychographics: An Aid to Demographics." *Adweek's Marketing Week* (September 11), p. 48.

Webber, Harry (1998). *Divide and Conquer: Target Your Customers Through Market Segmentation*. New York: John Wiley and Sons, Inc.

Weinstein, Art (1987). *Market Segmentation: Using Niche Marketing to Exploit New Markets*. Chicago, IL: Probus Publishing, Inc.

———. (1994). *Market Segmentation: Using Demographics, Psychographics and Other Niche Marketing Techniques to Predict Customer Behavior*, Revised Edition. Chicago, IL: Probus Publishing, Inc.

———. (2004). *Handbook of Market Segmentation: Strategic Targeting for Business and Technology Firms*, Third Edition. Binghamton, NY: The Haworth Press.

Weiss, Michael J. (1988) *The Clustering of America*. New York: Harper & Row.

———. (1994). *Latitudes and Attitudes: An Atlas of American Tastes, Trends, Politics, and Passions from Abilene, Texas, to Zanesville, Ohio*. Boston: Little, Brown and Co.

Wells, William D. (1975). "Psychographics: A Critical Review." *Journal of Marketing Research*, vol. 12 (May), pp. 196-213.

Wells, William D. and Geri Moore (1989). I Can Hear It, Coggins . . . America's Values Are Shifting Again. Paper presented at the American Marketing Association Attitude Research Conference, January 29-February 1.

West, Emily (2002). "Digital Sentiments: The 'Social Expression' Industry and New Technologies." *Journal of American and Comparative Cultures*, vol. 25, pp. 316-326.

Widgery, Robin and Jack McGaugh (1992). "When Women and Men Buy Cars." In Robert P. Leone and V. Kumar (eds.), *AMA Educators Proceedings* (pp. 117-118). Chicago, IL: American Marketing Association.

———. (1993). "Vehicle Message Appeals and the New Generation Woman." *Journal of Advertising Research* (September-October), pp. 36-42.

Wilkie, William L. and Joel B. Cohen (1977). "An Overview of Market Segmentation: Behavioral Concepts and Research Approaches" (working paper, pp. 77-105). Cambridge, MA: Marketing Science Institute.

Wilkins, Alan L. and W. Gibb Dyer Jr. (1988). "Toward Culturally Sensitive Theories of Cultural Change." *Academy of Management Review*, vol. 13, pp. 522-533.

Williams, Robin M. Jr. (1967). "Individual and Group Values." *Annals of the American Academy of Political and Social Science*, no. 371 (May), pp. 20-37.

———. (1979). "Change and Stability in Values and Value Systems: A Sociological Perspective." In Milton Rokeach (ed.), *Understanding Human Values: Individual and Societal* (pp. 20-37). New York: The Free Press.

Winters, Lewis C. (1989). "New Technologies: SRI Announces VALS2." *Marketing Research: A Magazine of Management & Applications* (June), pp. 67-69.

Witcher, Gregory (1988). "Car Ads Turn to High-Tech Talk—But Does Anybody Understand it?" *Wall Street Journal* (March 7), p. 21.

WJW-TV8 (1988). *Profiles for Advertising to Consumers Effectively.* Cleveland, OH: Marshall Marketing & Communications, Inc.

Zaslow, Jeffrey (2004). "Moving in with Your New Spouse—And Battling the Ghost of the Old One." *The Wall Street Journal* (September 16), p. D1.

Index

Lifestyle Market Segmentation
© 2006 by The Haworth Press, Inc. All rights reserved.
doi:10.1300/5560_28

Order a copy of this book with this form or online at:
http://www.haworthpress.com/store/product.asp?sku=5560

LIFESTYLE MARKET SEGMENTATION

_____ in hardbound at $34.95 (ISBN-13: 978-0-7890-2868-6; ISBN-10: 0-7890-2868-9)

_____ in softbound at $24.95 (ISBN-13: 978-0-7890-2869-3; ISBN-10: 0-7890-2869-7)

182 pages plus index • Includes illustrations

Or order online and use special offer code HEC25 in the shopping cart.

COST OF BOOKS_____	☐ **BILL ME LATER:** (Bill-me option is good on US/Canada/Mexico orders only; not good to jobbers, wholesalers, or subscription agencies.)
POSTAGE & HANDLING_____ *(US: $4.00 for first book & $1.50 for each additional book)* *(Outside US: $5.00 for first book & $2.00 for each additional book)*	☐ Check here if billing address is different from shipping address and attach purchase order and billing address information. Signature_____
SUBTOTAL_____	☐ **PAYMENT ENCLOSED: $_____**
IN CANADA: ADD 7% GST_____	☐ **PLEASE CHARGE TO MY CREDIT CARD.**
STATE TAX_____ *(NJ, NY, OH, MN, CA, IL, IN, PA, & SD residents, add appropriate local sales tax)*	☐ Visa ☐ MasterCard ☐ AmEx ☐ Discover ☐ Diner's Club ☐ Eurocard ☐ JCB Account # _____
FINAL TOTAL_____ *(If paying in Canadian funds, convert using the current exchange rate, UNESCO coupons welcome)*	Exp. Date_____ Signature_____

Prices in US dollars and subject to change without notice.

NAME_____

INSTITUTION_____

ADDRESS_____

CITY_____

STATE/ZIP_____

COUNTRY_____ COUNTY (NY residents only)_____

TEL_____ FAX_____

E-MAIL_____

May we use your e-mail address for confirmations and other types of information? ☐ Yes ☐ No
We appreciate receiving your e-mail address and fax number. Haworth would like to e-mail or fax special
discount offers to you, as a preferred customer. **We will never share, rent, or exchange your e-mail address
or fax number.** We regard such actions as an invasion of your privacy.

Order From Your Local Bookstore or Directly From
The Haworth Press, Inc.
10 Alice Street, Binghamton, New York 13904-1580 • USA
TELEPHONE: 1-800-HAWORTH (1-800-429-6784) / Outside US/Canada: (607) 722-5857
FAX: 1-800-895-0582 / Outside US/Canada: (607) 771-0012
E-mail to: orders@haworthpress.com

For orders outside US and Canada, you may wish to order through your local
sales representative, distributor, or bookseller.
For information, see http://haworthpress.com/distributors

(Discounts are available for individual orders in US and Canada only, not booksellers/distributors.)

PLEASE PHOTOCOPY THIS FORM FOR YOUR PERSONAL USE.
http://www.HaworthPress.com   BOF06